Land Animals

Joan S. Gottlieb

ISBN 0-7398-9177-4

7 8 9   1689   14 13 12

4500357004

Rigby · Steck-Vaughn

www.HarcourtAchieve.com
1.800.531.5015

Contents

UNIT 1
Animal Adaptations

Camel

Polar Bear

What Animals Need

Travel to a hot, dry desert. Visit a land frozen under ice. Go beneath the sea. In all these places you find animals. Animals live in almost every part of the world.

There are over one million kinds of animals. But all animals need many of the same things. They need food. Food gives them energy to live and grow. Animals need water. Some animals drink water. Others get water from the food they eat.

Many animals need shelter. A shelter is a place that protects an animal from the weather. It may be a place where an animal goes to escape an enemy. Some shelters keep young animals safe.

Animals get what they need from their **environment**. An environment is the place where an animal lives. The environment of a camel is the desert. A polar bear can be found in the cold Arctic.

Animals have special body parts that help them live in their environment. These body parts are called **adaptations**. Some adaptations help animals get food. Others help animals live in cold or hot places. Some protect an animal from its enemies.

Claws and teeth are two adaptations of a polar bear. These parts help a bear catch the seals it eats for food. A thick fur coat helps keep the bear warm. Could a polar bear live in a desert?

Animals get food in different ways. They have many ways to protect themselves. As you read, you will learn how different animals live in their environments.

A. Answer True or False.

1. Some animals do not need food. _____

2. Animals get what they need from their environment. _____

3. All animals live in the same environment. _____

4. Food gives animals energy to grow. _____

5. Some animals get water from the foods they eat. _____

6. A shelter may protect an animal from an enemy. _____

B. Write environment or adaptation next to each word or phrase.

1. desert _____

2. claws _____

3. sharp teeth _____

4. ocean _____

5. forest _____

6. thick coat of fur _____

C. Answer the questions.

1. Where do animals live? _____

_____

2. What are two things that all animals need to live? _____

_____

3. Why does an animal need shelter? _____

_____

_____

4. What are two adaptations of a polar bear? _____

_____

How Some Animals Get Food

White-Footed Mouse

Alaskan Brown Bear

Did you know that plants are food factories? Plants use materials from the soil, the energy of sunlight, air, and water to make their own food. Animals cannot make their food. They must get food from their environment.

Animals eat many kinds of food. Some animals eat only plants. These animals are **herbivores**. Horses, deer, mice, rabbits, and elephants are herbivores.

Herbivores have strong teeth to chew tough plant parts. Mice have teeth that never stop growing. So their teeth never wear out from chewing their food. These teeth are one of the adaptations of mice.

Some animals eat other animals. They are called **carnivores**. Tigers, foxes, and eagles are carnivores. Carnivores have adaptations to help them catch the animals they use as food. Many carnivores have sharp teeth and claws.

Most fish are carnivores. They eat worms, small water animals, and other fish.

A few kinds of carnivores eat only dead animals. These carnivores are called **scavengers.** A bird called a vulture is a scavenger. A vulture has good eyesight. It can see a dead animal from far away.

Some animals eat both plants and other animals. These animals are **omnivores**. Bears are omnivores. They use the claws on their big front paws to snatch a fish from a stream. They also eat berries, nuts, and fruits. Skunks and raccoons are omnivores, too. So are most people.

A. Find these words in the Glossary. Then write a definition for each.

1. omnivore _____

_____

2. herbivore _____

_____

3. carnivore _____

_____

4. scavenger _____

_____

B. Answer True or False.

1. A mouse is a carnivore. _____

2. Animals can make their own food. _____

3. Herbivores eat meat. _____

4. Special body parts help animals find and eat food. _____

C. Write carnivore, herbivore, or omnivore to answer each question.

1. What kind of animal eats other animals? _____

2. What kind of animal eats plants? _____

3. What kind of animal eats both plants and animals? _____

4. What kind of animal is a bear? _____

D. Answer the questions.

1. How are animals different from plants? _____

_____

_____

2. What adaptation does a vulture have to find food? _____

_____

How Birds Get Food

Sparrow

Hawk

Hummingbird

Woodpecker

Heron

Animals must get food from their environment. They have special body parts, or adaptations, to help them get their food.

Birds have some interesting adaptations. Their **beaks**, and sometimes their feet, help them get food. The shape and size of a beak can help tell you what the bird uses for food.

A sparrow has a beak that is short and strong. It feeds on the seeds of plants. It uses its beak to break open the seeds. Sparrows are found in almost every environment in the United States.

A hawk uses both its claws and its beak to get food. It can catch a mouse or a snake in its claws. Then it uses its sharp, curved beak to cut and tear the meat.

Hummingbirds feed on **nectar**, a sweet liquid inside a flower. The hummingbird's beak is long and thin. It can reach the inside of the flower to get to the nectar.

Hummingbirds have another adaptation. While they are feeding, they move their tiny wings in a circle. This helps them hang in the air, like a helicopter.

Have you ever heard the sound that a woodpecker makes? With its strong beak, a woodpecker makes holes in the bark of trees. Then it eats the insects and the other small animals that it pulls out of the holes.

Birds such as herons have long legs for wading in water. They use their long, pointed beaks to catch fish and frogs. Could a heron live in a desert?

A. Draw lines between the bird and its special adaptations.

1. hawk   short, strong beak for opening seeds

2. hummingbird   long beak for catching fish and frogs

3. heron   long, thin beak and special wings

4. woodpecker   sharp, curved beak and claws

5. sparrow   strong beak for making holes in trees

B. Complete each of the following sentences. Use the words below.

adaptations	beaks	environment	foods

1. Animals get their food from their _____.

2. The special body parts of animals are called _____.

3. Animals have different adaptations because they eat

   different _____.

4. Most birds use their _____ to help them get food.

C. Answer the questions.

1. What does a hawk use to get food? _____

   _____

   _____

2. How is a sparrow's beak different from a heron's beak? _____

   _____

   _____

3. What kind of food does a woodpecker eat? _____

   _____

4. Why do birds have beaks of different shapes and sizes? _____

   _____

Safe in the Environment

Harbor Seals

You have read about some of the adaptations that animals have for getting food. Now read about other adaptations that animals have to help them stay alive in their environment.

Some seals live in the Arctic. They have thick layers of fat to help keep them warm. Remember that polar bears live in the Arctic, too. They have layers of fat and a thick fur coat to help keep them warm. Polar bears are well protected by their fat and fur. They can even swim in icy cold Arctic waters.

The desert is very hot and has little or no water. Many desert animals, such as lizards and gerbils, spend the hottest part of the day in holes they have dug. They come out at night when it is cooler. They can also go for a long time without drinking water. Some desert animals get the water they need from the plants or animals they eat.

Many birds that nest in the north do not stay there through the cold winter. These birds **migrate**, or travel south to warmer areas where they can find food. In the spring they return north. This two-way trip is called **migration**.

Woodchucks and bears can't find food during the winter. So they eat all summer and fall until they get very fat. Then they sleep or rest through the winter in holes or caves. This sleep is called **hibernation.** Some desert animals have a similar adaptation. They sleep through hot or very dry times.

A. Find these words in the Glossary. Then write a definition for each.

1. adaptation _____

_____

2. migration _____

_____

3. hibernation _____

_____

B. Complete each sentence.

1. A polar bear's fat and fur help it to _____.

2. A desert animal escapes the heat by spending the day _____.

3. When the weather gets cold, many birds _____.

4. The desert is hot during the day and cooler at _____.

C. Answer True or False.

1. Many birds hibernate. _____

2. Lizards have a layer of fat to keep them warm. _____

3. Birds migrate to the south in the summer. _____

4. An adaptation helps an animal live in its environment. _____

5. Seals hibernate during the winter. _____

D. Answer the questions.

1. Why do woodchucks hibernate? _____

_____

2. Why do some birds migrate south in the winter? _____

_____

3. What adaptation does a seal have for living in the Arctic? _____

_____

Safe from Enemies

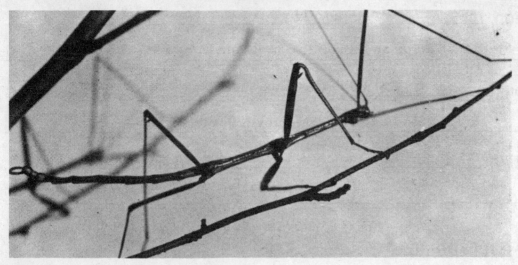

Can you see the insect in this picture?

Many animals are in danger from other animals. They must protect themselves from being caught and eaten.

Some animals are hard for an enemy to see. Their colors help them blend in with their environment. This protective coloring is called **camouflage**. Some lizards and snakes that live in trees are green. They blend in with the color of the leaves. Some insects that live on tree branches are brown. They match the color of tree bark.

Deer have long legs and can run fast. They use speed to get away from an enemy.

Some animals use sprays to protect themselves. The spray from a skunk has a very bad smell. Most animals run away from it! A horned lizard can spray blood from its eyes into an enemy's eyes. While its enemy has trouble seeing, the lizard can escape.

Some animals have weapons. A porcupine has sharp quills on its body. Anything that attacks the porcupine gets stuck with the quills.

Poison is another weapon that animals can use. Bees and wasps have stings that are poisonous. The bite of a rattlesnake is poisonous, too. Some toads have a poison on their skin. Any animal that tries to eat the toad will get sick.

A. Choose a word from below that matches the way an animal protects itself.

camouflage	poison	quills	spray

1. horned lizard _____

2. porcupine _____

3. bees _____

4. toad _____

5. skunk _____

6. green tree snake _____

B. Fill in the missing word.

1. Protective coloring is called _____. (camouflage, poison)

2. A skunk uses a _____ to protect itself. (poison, spray)

3. A green tree snake is protected by _____. (poison, camouflage)

4. A porcupine protects itself with _____. (quills, poison)

5. Camouflage means that an animal's color helps it blend in with its _____. (enemies, environment)

C. Answer the questions.

1. What are two ways that animals can protect themselves? _____

_____

_____

2. What happens to an animal that attacks a porcupine? _____

_____

3. How does camouflage protect an animal from enemies? _____

_____

Animal Homes

A Beaver Lodge

Animals need shelter from bad weather and from other animals. Some animals use trees, caves, or holes in the ground. But others build their homes.

Many animals dig holes in the ground. In the hole, an animal can stay warm in winter and cool in summer. A hole also keeps larger animals out. Rabbits, mice, and chipmunks dig holes for homes. Foxes also dig holes. A fox hole is called a **den**. The den protects the young foxes from other animals.

Prairie dogs are small animals in the squirrel family. These animals dig a long hole in the ground called a **burrow**. They sleep and store food in the burrow. During the day, prairie dogs leave the burrow to look for food. But if they see an enemy, they run back to the burrow to hide.

The beaver builds a home in the water. It is called a **lodge**. The beaver uses its sharp front teeth to cut down trees. It uses the tree bark for food. It uses the trunk of the tree to build the lodge. Inside its home, a family of beavers is safe from animals that might use the beavers as food.

Deer do not have homes. They move around in groups for safety. Monkeys also travel in groups for safety. At night most monkeys sleep in trees. They build nests of leaves to sleep in each night.

A. Choose a word or phrase to match each animal with its home.

burrow	does not have a home	lodge
den	sleeps in a tree	

1. prairie dog _____

2. deer _____

3. monkey _____

4. fox _____

5. beaver _____

B. Answer <u>True</u> or <u>False</u>.

1. All animals live in the same kind of shelter. _____

2. A den protects young foxes. _____

3. Many animals dig holes in the ground to stay warm in winter and cool in summer. _____

4. Some monkeys make nests in trees. _____

5. A beaver builds a home with rocks. _____

C. Answer the questions.

1. Where do beavers build their lodges? _____

_____

2. How do deer stay safe? _____

_____

3. How does a den protect young foxes? _____

_____

4. Why do animals need shelter? _____

_____

Young Animals

A Yellowhammer Feeding
Its Young

All animals **reproduce**. They make more living things like themselves. Some animals, like birds and insects, lay eggs. Other animals, like cats and horses, reproduce and then give birth to live young.

Most fish, insects, and snakes can find their own food soon after they are born. Other young animals are fed and protected by their parents.

Young birds grow up in nests that are built by the parent birds. The parents will feed the young birds until they are strong enough to fly.

Some animals, like wolves, live in large groups called **packs**. All the adults in the pack help feed and protect the young wolves. Young wolves learn the skills they will need to survive by watching the adults and playing with each other.

A. Answer True or False.

1. All young animals need their parents. _____

2. Young wolves grow up on their own. _____

3. Young birds are fed by their parents. _____

B. Answer the questions.

1. What are three kinds of animals that can find their own food soon after they are born? _____

_____

2. When do parent birds stop feeding their young? _____

_____

Part A

Read each sentence. Write <u>True</u> if the sentence is true and <u>False</u> if it is false.

1. Food gives animals energy to live and grow. _____

2. All animals need food and water. _____

3. The place where an animal lives is its environment. _____

4. A tiger's claws and a seal's fat are both adaptations. _____

5. Animals can make their own food. _____

6. A horned lizard sprays blood into an enemy's eyes. _____

7. Herbivores eat only dead animals. _____

8. A sparrow's thick beak helps it to catch other animals. _____

9. A porcupine uses its bad-smelling spray as a weapon. _____

10. A beaver builds a lodge as a shelter. _____

Part B

Write the word that best completes each sentence. Use the words below.

adaptation	herbivore	migration
camouflage	hibernation	omnivore
carnivore		

1. An animal that eats only other animals is a _____.

2. Traveling to a warmer area to find food is called _____.

3. A body part that helps an animal live is an _____.

4. During _____ an animal sleeps through the winter.

5. An animal that eats both plants and animals is an _____.

6. Coloring that helps an animal blend in with its environment is

   called _____.

Find Animal Adaptations

You Need

- drawing paper
- crayons or markers
- 2 to 4 labels

1. Look at the picture here. The Gila monster in its environment has been done as an example.

2. Choose another animal. The animal may be real, or you can invent one.

3. Think about your animal's adaptations
   - for getting food.
   - for keeping safe in its environment.
   - for keeping safe from enemies.

4. Draw a picture of your animal in its environment. Include its food or its enemies in your drawing.

5. Use the labels to point out at least two adaptations. Use a different label for each adaptation. Write the name of your animal on another label. Put the labels on your drawing.

Gila Monster

Hole for hot time of day

Poisonous Bite

Protective Coloring

Write the Answer
Describe how adaptations help your animal get food or keep safe.

_____

_____

_____

Fill in the circle in front of the word or phrase that best completes each sentence. The first one is done for you.

1. To sleep or rest through the winter is called
   ● hibernation.
   ⓑ reproduction.
   ⓒ migration.

2. With its coloring a green tree snake can
   ⓐ make food.
   ⓑ hibernate.
   ⓒ hide from its enemies.

3. An animal reproduces by
   ⓐ making a nest.
   ⓑ making more living things like itself.
   ⓒ migrating.

4. An animal that eats only other animals is called a
   ⓐ migration.
   ⓑ carnivore.
   ⓒ horse.

5. A bear hibernates because it
   ⓐ can't find food in winter.
   ⓑ is very tired.
   ⓒ has too much fat.

6. A hawk uses claws to
   ⓐ dig holes in the ground.
   ⓑ catch its food.
   ⓒ hide from enemies.

Fill in the missing words.

7. Birds migrate to _____ . (find food, get exercise)

8. A young snake can _____ .
   (find its own food, make a nest)

9. The Arctic is the environment of a _____ .
   (camel, polar bear)

Write the answer on the lines.

10. What are two things that all animals need to live?

_____

_____

UNIT 2
Invertebrate Animals

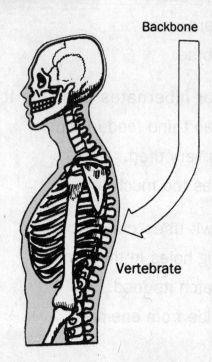

Backbone

Vertebrate

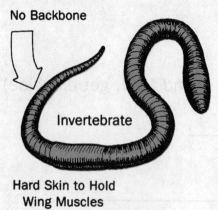

No Backbone

Invertebrate

Hard Skin to Hold Wing Muscles

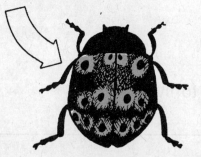

Invertebrate

What Is an Invertebrate?

Invertebrates are animals that do not have backbones. Worms, spiders, flies, and many other animals are invertebrates. People, horses, and cats are different. They have backbones. They are called **vertebrates.** Birds, fish, snakes, and frogs are also vertebrates.

There are more kinds of invertebrates than vertebrates. Most invertebrates are smaller than vertebrates. For example, a fly is smaller than a cat. Many invertebrates and vertebrates live on land. Worms, spiders, and insects are some invertebrates that live on land.

Invertebrates do not have backbones. So how do their bodies keep their shape? The inside of a worm's body presses out on the skin. In insects and some other invertebrates, the skin is hard. Muscles are attached to the skin. Flying insects have many wing muscles.

Invertebrates get the air they need in different ways. Worms take in air through their skin. Insects and spiders take in air through air pipes on their body.

Animals need food to grow. Their bodies break down food into tiny pieces. Blood carries the tiny pieces around the body. In invertebrates, blood goes through tubes and spaces in the body. The heart helps the blood move. Some invertebrates have more than one heart.

An invertebrate must get rid of its skin in order to grow. A chemical in its body helps the animal do this.

A. Answer True or False.

1. Animals without backbones are called vertebrates. _____

2. You can find both vertebrates and invertebrates on land. _____

3. Even though a fly is small, it still has a backbone. _____

4. Flying insects use wing muscles to fly. _____

5. Insects and spiders take in air through their mouth. _____

6. An invertebrate must get rid of its skin in order to grow. _____

7. People are vertebrates. _____

8. Some invertebrates have more than one heart. _____

B. Write the letter for the correct answer.

1. All these animals are invertebrates except _____.
   (a) worms   (b) flies   (c) dogs   (d) spiders

2. Most invertebrates are _____ than vertebrates.
   (a) larger   (b) redder   (c) softer   (d) smaller

3. An invertebrate you might find in a garden is a _____.
   (a) horse   (b) cat   (c) worm   (d) fish

4. When an animal gets rid of its skin, it is trying to _____.
   (a) grow   (b) change color   (c) hide   (d) lay eggs

C. Use each word to write a sentence about animals.

1. invertebrates _____

_____

2. vertebrates _____

_____

3. worms _____

_____

4. muscles _____

_____

21

Earthworms

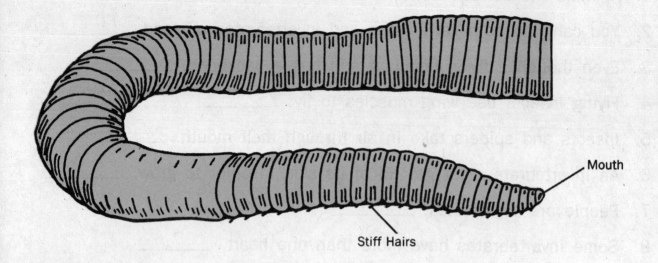

Mouth

Stiff Hairs

Have you ever seen a robin tug at an earthworm? It must pull very hard. The earthworm uses its stiff hairs to hold on under the ground. The stiff hairs are attached to muscles.

Earthworms do not have eyes or ears. But they do have special mouths. Their mouths are sensitive to heat, light, and touch. Earthworms have 10 hearts.

There are more than 2,200 different kinds of earthworms. They can be as short as 1 inch or as long as 11 feet. Earthworms are found all over the world except in very dry or very cold places.

Earthworms live under the ground in wet soil. They come to the surface only at night. Then they crawl around, looking for dead plants to eat. This is why they are called "night crawlers." An earthworm crawls by stretching the front of its body forward. As it does this, it pulls up the back of its body.

An earthworm spends the day under the surface of the soil. It digs tunnels through the soil. This activity of earthworms is very important to people. Without earthworms, unplowed land would be hard and useless. Earthworms mix the soil. The tunnels they make let air and water into the soil. The wastes from earthworms help make the soil rich. This light, rich soil is called topsoil. Plants grow well in topsoil.

A. Complete the sentences. Use the words below.

day	dry	topsoil
digging	hairs	wet

1. Earthworms have stiff _____ that help them hold on to the soil.

2. To find earthworms during the _____, you must dig them up.

3. Earthworms live under the ground, in soil that is _____.

4. Earthworms make soil light by _____ tunnels into the ground.

5. Plants grow well in the _____ made by earthworms.

B. Answer True or False.

1. Some earthworms are as long as 11 feet. _____

2. Earthworms live in places that are dry and cold. _____

3. Earthworms move slowly because their legs are tiny. _____

4. Because they mix the soil, earthworms harm the soil. _____

5. Earthworms do not have eyes or ears. _____

6. Earthworms come to the surface of the soil at night. _____

C. Answer the questions.

1. Why are earthworms called "night crawlers"? _____

_____

2. What do earthworms eat? _____

3. How many hearts does an earthworm have? _____

4. What is topsoil? _____

_____

5. How do earthworms move? _____

_____

_____

Spiders

Orange Garden Spider

Some spiders walk thousands of feet in the air on a silk thread. Why don't they just fly like other insects? Spiders do not have wings. And they are not insects. Insects have 3 pairs of legs. Spiders have 4 pairs. A spider uses its 8 legs to learn what is happening around it. An insect uses a pair of feelers. Insects are omnivores. They eat both plants and animals. Spiders are carnivores. They eat insects.

Some spiders spin webs to trap the insects they use as food. Webs are made of silk that comes from the spider's body. A different kind of silk is used to make egg sacs. The female lays eggs and wraps them in the silk sac. After the eggs hatch, the young stay in the sac until they get strong.

Spiders live anywhere they can find food. There are thousands of different kinds of spiders. Some are smaller than the period at the end of this sentence. But the bird-eating spider of South America has a 3-inch body and 4-inch long legs.

In the United States, there are a few spiders that are dangerous to people. Two of these are the female **black widow** and the **brown recluse.**

Most spiders are valuable to people. They eat insects, such as beetles and grasshoppers, that may harm food plants.

A. Complete each sentence.

1. Spiders have _____ pairs of legs.

2. Some spiders get their food by _____.

3. Webs and egg sacs are both made of _____.

4. Two spiders that are dangerous to people are the _____

_____.

5. Spiders are valuable because they eat harmful _____.

B. Use each word to write a sentence about spiders.

1. spiders _____

_____

2. web _____

_____

3. silk _____

_____

4. black widow _____

_____

C. Answer True or False.

1. Spiders cannot fly. _____

2. Insects have fewer legs than spiders. _____

3. Some spiders make webs. _____

4. The bites of all spiders kill people. _____

5. Most spiders are helpful to people. _____

6. Spiders eat some insects that harm food plants. _____

7. Most spiders are carnivores. _____

8. Female spiders lay eggs. _____

Cockroaches

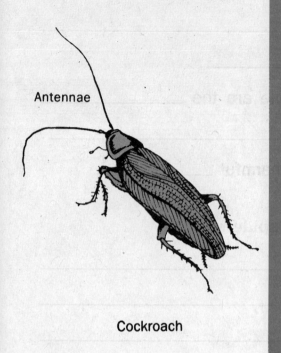

Antennae

Cockroach

Cockroaches are insects. There are many kinds of cockroaches. Some kinds can fly. Roaches are kitchen pests in warm climates. They leave many droppings, or wastes. Cockroaches can carry germs. As far as we know, cockroaches do not spread disease.

Roaches come out at night. They use **antennae,** or feelers, for a sense of touch and smell. They will eat any kind of food. They also eat paper, cloth, ink, and even shoe polish.

The German cockroach is found all over the world. This cockroach is about ½ inch long. It is yellow-brown and has wings. The American cockroach is about 1½ inches long. It is brown and can fly.

Keeping cockroaches out of houses is not easy. The best way is to keep the kitchen clean. Wash dishes before going to bed. Don't leave food around. Don't leave paper bags in corners where cockroaches can hide.

A. **Write the letter for the correct answer.**

1. Roaches hunt for food in the _____.
   (a) morning   (b) summer   (c) night   (d) rain

2. All of these are food for roaches except _____.
   (a) ink   (b) rocks   (c) pet food   (d) bread

B. **Answer the questions.**

1. Where is the German cockroach found? _____

_____

2. What do roaches smell with? _____

Termites

Termites are insects that live in large groups called **colonies.** Each colony is started by a **king** and a **queen.** After they mate, the queen grows much larger. A queen termite can lay 10,000 eggs a day!

Other kinds of termites cannot mate. The small, blind **worker** termites do all the work in the colony. They build tunnels and feed the other termites. The **soldier** termites are also blind. Soldiers defend the colony against attack by ants or other enemies.

In warm climates, termites build huge nests called **mounds.** A mound is made of bits of dirt mixed with termite saliva. In the United States, most termites live underground. The workers chew tunnels through the wood of buildings. Because termites can do great harm to buildings, they are serious pests.

Termites

Termite Mound

A. Answer True or False.

1. All termites can mate and lay eggs. _____

2. Soldier termites defend the colony. _____

3. Termites can chew through stone. _____

B. Answer the questions.

1. What kinds of termites live in a colony? _____

_____

_____

2. Why are termites serious pests? _____

_____

Beetles

Firefly

Ladybug

Imagine a family with 300,000 relatives! That is how many different kinds of beetles there are. The beetle family is bigger than any other animal family.

Beetles are insects. Most beetles can fly. They have 2 pairs of wings. One pair is thin and light. This pair is used for flying. The second pair is made of a hard material. This material protects the thin flying wings. The outer wings of most beetles are brightly colored.

Beetles can live almost anywhere. Some live in water. Others live on the ground. Some make their homes in the soil.

You may know about some beetles. Fireflies are beetles. Look for these insects on a summer night. They give off a soft, green light.

Ladybugs are beetles, too. They are helpful. They eat other insects that harm plants.

Some beetles are pests. They harm plants used for food. With their strong jaws, they can bite through plants. Japanese beetles destroy trees and crops. Other beetles feed on grain. Some beetles live in houses. They feed on cloth, rugs, and food.

A. Fill in the missing words.

1. Beetles are _____. (crops, insects)

2. Beetles have _____ wings. (4, 6)

3. Beetles use _____ wings for flying. (2, all)

4. Japanese beetles are _____ insects. (helpful, harmful)

5. Ladybugs are _____ beetles. (helpful, harmful)

6. Beetles eat _____. (only other insects, many things)

B. Answer True or False.

1. There are many kinds of beetles. _____

2. No beetles can fly. _____

3. Beetles have 2 pairs of wings. _____

4. Fireflies are beetles. _____

5. Spiders are beetles. _____

6. All beetles live in the water. _____

C. Answer the questions.

1. What do the outer wings of most beetles look like? _____
_____

2. How many pairs of wings do most beetles have? _____
_____

3. How are ladybugs helpful to people? _____
_____

4. How are Japanese beetles harmful to people? _____
_____

5. How can you find a firefly on a summer night? _____
_____

Ants

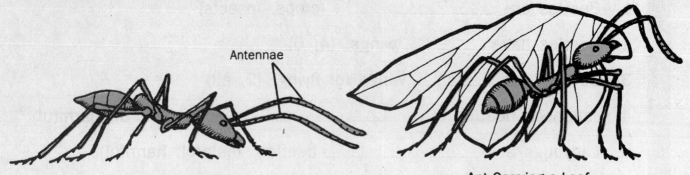

Antennae

Ant Carrying a Leaf

Ants are insects that live in colonies. They make nests underground or in dead wood. One nest may hold a few ants or a million. A female ant, young ants, and workers live in each nest.

Every ant has a job. Ants that can mate have wings. The male and female fly into the air to mate. Then the male dies. The female loses her wings and lays eggs. The female is called a queen.

Females that cannot mate are workers. Workers bring food into the nest. They clean the nest and take care of the young. Some workers are soldiers. They keep enemies out of the nest.

Ants remember how things smell and feel. This helps them tell an enemy from a friend. It also helps them find the path to their nest. Ants know what is around them by touching things with two antennae, the feelers on their heads. Ants also have hundreds of tiny eyes that make up one large **compound eye.** Compound eyes help ants see what is moving around them.

Army ants live in South America and the southern United States. They travel from place to place to find food. Army ants eat insects and spiders. But they can also kill and eat lizards or snakes.

Army ants do not build nests. When they stop to rest, millions of ants cling together in a huge ball. Each ant holds on to the legs of another ant. Inside the ball are the queen and her young.

A. Answer True or False.

1. The job of the queen ant is to gather food. _____

2. After a female ant lays eggs, it becomes a worker. _____

3. Antennae are the feelers on an ant's head. _____

4. Ants cannot see. _____

B. Write the letter for the correct answer.

1. Ants make their homes in _____.
   (a) buildings   (b) the ground   (c) water   (d) cellars

2. Worker ants do all of these jobs except _____.
   (a) cleaning up   (b) laying eggs
   (c) defending the nest   (d) finding food

3. The ant that lays eggs in a nest is called the _____.
   (a) male   (b) worker   (c) queen   (d) baby

4. An ant can tell if its enemy is near by the enemy's _____.
   (a) sounds   (b) looks   (c) taste   (d) smell

C. Complete each sentence.

1. Ants are insects that live in _____.

2. The ants that bring food to the nest are called _____.

3. Some worker ants, called _____ keep enemies out of the nest.

4. Ants know what is around them by touching things with their two

   _____.

D. Answer the questions.

1. Where do ants build their nests? _____

   _____

2. What do army ants eat? _____

   _____

   _____

Bees

Worker

Queen

Drone

Workers store nectar and pollen in the combs.

Could you tell someone the way to the grocery store by dancing? Bees dance to show other bees where food is. The dances even tell how far away the food is. Bees find food inside flowers.

Bees are useful insects. They make the honey that people use as food. They also make wax. Beeswax is made into candles and other products.

There are many kinds of bees. **Honeybees** make the honey and wax that people can use. Honeybees live in a nest called a **hive.** A hive has many rooms with 6 sides. The rooms are made of wax. A group of rooms is called a **comb.**

Each hive has a queen. She is the largest bee. She mates with the male bees, called **drones.** Then she lays eggs for the rest of her life.

Most of the bees in a hive are workers. Workers do most of the jobs. They build the hive. They look for food. When they find flowers, they dance to show others where the food is. Then many workers fly to the flowers to feed. They collect nectar and **pollen** from the flowers. The nectar turns to honey in the stomach of a bee. The workers store the honey and pollen in the combs. This is food for young bees, the queen, and the drones.

As they feed, bees carry pollen from one flower to another. Pollen helps flowers make seeds. This is another way in which bees are useful.

A. **Answer True or False.**

1. Bees sing to tell each other where to find food. _____

2. Honeybees make honey and wax. _____

3. Honey is stored in the combs. _____

4. The queen lays eggs. _____

5. Drones get food for the young bees. _____

6. Workers collect nectar and pollen from flowers. _____

7. Bees find their food inside flowers. _____

8. Wax turns to honey in the stomach of a bee. _____

B. **Use each word to write a sentence about bees.**

1. hive _____

_____

2. queen _____

_____

3. nectar _____

_____

C. **Fill in the missing words.**

1. Honeybees make _____ and honey. (wax, pollen)

2. Each room in a comb has _____ sides. (6, 16)

3. Nectar turns to _____ in the stomach of a worker bee. (wax, honey)

4. Male bees are called _____. (drones, workers)

5. The largest bee in a hive is the _____. (king, queen)

6. As they feed, bees carry _____ from flower to flower. (wax, pollen)

7. Bees _____ to show other bees where food is. (sing, dance)

33

Butterflies and Moths

Monarch Butterfly

Moth

Caterpillar

Cocoon

You see an insect with colorful wings resting on a flower. Is it a butterfly or a moth? If you see it during the day, it is probably a butterfly. Most moths fly only at night. A butterfly's body is thin and smooth. A moth's body is thick and furry. Butterflies hold their wings straight up. Moths spread their wings out flat.

But butterflies and moths are alike in two ways. Both have wings covered with colorful **scales.** Both have long, rolled-up tongues. They use their tongues to drink nectar from flowers. As they feed, they carry pollen from one flower to another. This helps seeds and fruit to grow.

Female moths and butterflies lay eggs on leaves or stems. The eggs hatch into **caterpillars.** A caterpillar looks like a worm. Its most important job is to eat. Caterpillars feed mostly on leaves. In fact, a tree may die if caterpillars eat many of its leaves.

Caterpillars that become moths change inside a **cocoon** of silk. The silkworm moth makes its cocoon from one silk thread that is 1,000 yards long. People use this thread to make silk cloth.

Most caterpillars that become butterflies do not make a cocoon. Instead the skin becomes a hard case. The caterpillar becomes a **pupa.** Inside the pupa, wings grow. Soon an adult butterfly comes out.

A. Write the correct label on the diagram.

1. _____

2. _____

_____   _____

B. Answer True or False.

1. Butterflies fly at night. _____

2. Butterflies and moths find food in flowers. _____

3. Caterpillars eat the leaves of trees. _____

4. A young moth looks like its parents, only smaller. _____

5. A moth's body is thick and furry. _____

C. Complete each sentence.

1. A butterfly sticks its _____ into a flower to drink.

2. Butterflies and moths help _____ and _____ grow.

3. One kind of caterpillar makes _____ used for cloth.

4. The female lays _____ on leaves or stems.

D. Use each word to write a sentence about butterflies and moths.

1. moth _____

_____

2. caterpillar _____

_____

3. cocoon _____

_____

Mosquitoes

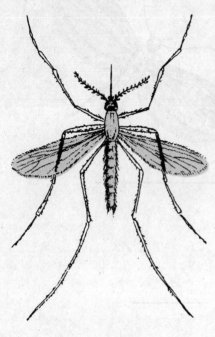

Adult Mosquito

Something bites your arm. A bump starts to grow. It itches. What insect did that? Probably a mosquito. There are more than 3,000 kinds of mosquitoes. They are found all over the world. Most mosquitoes are about ¼ inch long. They each have 1 pair of wings.

Most mosquitoes lay their eggs on water. The eggs float. They hatch into **larvae.** The larvae look like worms. When they grow, their skin comes off. Then mosquitoes with wings fly out.

To find a female, the male uses its antennae to pick up the sound of the female's wings. After they mate, the male dies.

Only female mosquitoes bite. The female needs to feed on blood to make eggs. Some kinds of mosquitoes feed only on frogs or snakes. Others feed on cows, horses, and people.

A. Use each word to write a sentence about mosquitoes.

1. larvae _____

_____

2. blood _____

_____

B. Answer the questions.

1. How does the male mosquito find the female? _____

_____

2. Where do mosquitoes lay eggs? _____

UNIT 2 Review

Part A

Read each sentence. Write **True** if the sentence is true and **False** if it is false.

1. Because invertebrates are small, they have small backbones. _____

2. Earthworms come out of the ground at night. _____

3. The queen bee's job is to keep the nest clean. _____

4. Spiders are invertebrates, but they are not insects. _____

5. The bodies of butterflies and moths look the same. _____

6. Ants live in groups called colonies. _____

7. Most beetles have 2 pairs of wings, but they use only 1 pair to fly.

    _____

8. Termites can chew tunnels through wood. _____

Part B

Fill in the missing word in each sentence. Use the words below.

butterflies	invertebrates	spiders
cockroach	moth	vertebrates
eyes	soil	workers

1. Earthworms mix the _____ so plants grow better in it.

2. Some _____ catch their food in webs.

3. A major kitchen pest is the _____.

4. Animals without backbones are called _____.

5. Ants have compound _____.

6. Inside a cocoon, a caterpillar changes into a _____.

7. Honeybee _____ make honey and wax.

EXPLORE & DISCOVER

Make a Model Insect

You Need

- pictures of insects
- 3 plastic foam balls
- 7 to 8 pipe cleaners
- old greeting cards or tagboard
- scissors
- markers

1. Make a model of an insect. Use three plastic foam balls for its main body parts. Push a pipe cleaner through the center of the balls to join them together. Cut off any extra piece of the pipe cleaner.

2. Use pipe cleaners to make six legs for your insect. Which body part should you attach the legs to? Look at a picture to help you.

3. Does your insect have antennae? If so, cut a pipe cleaner in half to make antennae.

4. Does your insect have wings? You can make colorful wings from old greeting cards. Or you can use tagboard and color it with markers. Cut sharp points to attach the wings to the body as shown.

5. Use markers to add eyes, mouthparts, and other coloring to your insect.

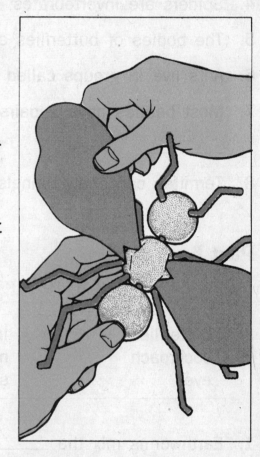

Write the Answer

Compare your model insect with those of your classmates. How are they all alike? What are some differences?

_____

_____

_____

Fill in the circle in front of the word or phrase that best completes each sentence. The first one is done for you.

1. An example of an invertebrate is a
    ⓐ frog.
    ⓑ snake.
    ● butterfly.

2. A large termite group is called a
    ⓐ colony.
    ⓑ hive.
    ⓒ burrow.

3. The German cockroach is found
    ⓐ only in Germany.
    ⓑ all over the world.
    ⓒ only in the Arctic.

4. A kind of beetle is the
    ⓐ honeybee.
    ⓑ black widow spider.
    ⓒ ladybug.

5. Caterpillars eat
    ⓐ nectar.
    ⓑ meat.
    ⓒ leaves.

6. Ants learn what is around them by touching things with their
    ⓐ antennae.
    ⓑ feet.
    ⓒ tails.

Fill in the missing words.

7. An animal that must get rid of its skin in order to grow is
    _____. (an invertebrate, a vertebrate)

8. Earthworms help make soil _____. (hard, rich)

9. An earthworm's body has _____.
    (stiff hairs, eyes)

Write the answer on the lines.

10. Why do certain female mosquitoes bite people?

    _____

    _____

UNIT 3
Amphibians

Egg

Tadpole

Adult Frog

What Is an Amphibian?

Think of three animals. You probably thought of vertebrates. A vertebrate is an animal with a backbone. A giraffe is a vertebrate. So is a dog, an ape, and a moose.

One group of vertebrate animals is the **amphibians.** Amphibians include frogs, toads, and salamanders. Amphibians are **cold-blooded** animals. Cold-blooded means an animal's body temperature changes as the outside temperature changes. The temperature of your body always stays the same. Even if you are outside on a cold day, your body temperature is 98.6 degrees Fahrenheit.

When amphibians reproduce, they lay eggs. Most lay eggs in water. The young that hatch live in the water. This is the first stage in the life of an amphibian. The young breathe with **gills.** Gills are body parts that take air out of water.

When amphibians are adults, they live on land. This is the second stage of their lives. On land, amphibians breathe air with lungs. Most amphibians also take in air through their skin. To be able to do this, the skin must be moist. So amphibians are found near water or in wet places.

A young frog is called a **tadpole.** It looks very different from its parents. A tadpole has gills and a tail. It does not have legs. As it grows the tadpole loses its gills and grows lungs. It loses its tail and grows legs. When these changes are over, the tadpole leaves the water and lives on land. It is now an adult frog.

A. Draw lines to complete the sentences.

1. Amphibians are   breathe in water.

2. Amphibians are found in   cold-blooded.

3. A tadpole uses gills to   wet places.

4. When amphibians reproduce, they   an adult.

5. A frog with lungs is   lay eggs.

B. Use the words below to complete the sentences.

gills	lungs	tadpole	vertebrate

1. An animal with a backbone is a _____.

2. Most adult amphibians breathe with _____.

3. Young amphibians breathe in water with _____.

4. A frog with gills is called a _____.

C. Answer the questions.

1. What group of animals do amphibians belong to? _____

2. When amphibians reproduce, what do they do? _____

_____

3. Where do young amphibians live? _____

4. What do most adult amphibians use to breathe? _____

5. What is a tadpole? _____

6. What does being a cold-blooded animal mean? _____

_____

_____

7. What three kinds of animals are in the amphibian group? _____

_____

Frogs

Bullfrog

Leopard Frog

Frogs live in most parts of the world. You can find frogs in most ponds, lakes, and streams.

Frogs move by jumping. The back legs of a frog are longer than its front legs. These long, strong legs help the frog jump. When a frog is scared, it often jumps back into the water. In the water, frogs are very good swimmers. Their toes have webs of skin between them that help them swim.

A frog has a long, sticky tongue that it uses to get food. Frogs eat insects. When a frog sees an insect, it shoots out its tongue and hits the insect with it. The insect sticks to the tongue! Then the frog pulls back its tongue and swallows its meal.

Male frogs make a loud croaking sound to attract females. They fill their lungs with air and then force the air out. Each kind of frog has its own special call.

One of the biggest frogs in the world is the bullfrog. Bullfrogs can grow to be 8 inches long. They eat mostly insects. But because they are so large, they can catch mice, bats, and even other frogs.

Most frogs have thin, moist skin. Many frogs have a poison in their skin. This poison protects them from being eaten by other animals. An animal that gets a taste of the poison usually drops the frog.

Frogs are useful to people because of the huge number of insects they eat. Without frogs, insects could become pests in many places.

A. Answer <u>True</u> or <u>False</u>.

1. Frogs eat mostly insects. _____

2. Frogs move by walking. _____

3. Frogs have webbed feet. _____

4. When a frog is scared, it jumps into a hole. _____

5. The back legs of a frog are used for jumping. _____

6. Most frogs lay their eggs in water. _____

7. Frogs are found only in warm countries. _____

B. Complete the sentences.

1. In the water, frogs are very good _____.

2. Most frogs are found near _____.

3. To attract females, male frogs make a _____

   _____.

4. Bullfrogs are so large that they can eat _____

   _____.

5. Frogs are useful to people because they _____.

C. Answer the questions.

1. What body part helps a frog swim? _____

   _____

2. What do most frogs eat? _____

3. How does a frog catch its food? _____

   _____

4. How are many frogs protected from their enemies? _____

   _____

43

Toads

Toads have rough, dry skin with bumps.

Toad Catching Insect

Toads are like frogs in some ways. Toads lay their eggs in water. The young that hatch from the eggs are tadpoles.

Toads move by jumping. They have a long, sticky tongue for catching insects. The males make a croaking noise to attract females.

Toads are different from frogs in some ways. The back legs of a toad are not as large as those of a frog. Frogs have smooth skin. Toads have rough, dry skin with bumps. Toads spend more time on land than frogs. Many toads only go into the water to lay eggs.

Some toads live in the hot desert. To escape the heat, toads stay in holes in the ground. A toad may stay in its hole for almost a year. It will come out when it rains. Then the toad will lay its eggs in rain puddles. The tadpoles that hatch from the eggs become adults before the sun dries up the puddles. When the water is gone, the toads go back to their holes. They won't come out until the next rain.

Most toads live in forests and gardens. People find toads helpful because they eat insects that can harm garden plants.

Some people believe that you can get warts from touching a toad. This story is not true. Toads do have a poison in their skin. But you can't be harmed by the poison. The poison bothers some animals that try to eat the toad. Snakes and raccoons are not bothered by the poison. Raccoons roll toads on the ground to rub the poison off. Then they eat the toads.

A. Answer True or False.

1. Toads are amphibians. _____

2. Young toads are tadpoles. _____

3. Toads have long, sticky tongues. _____

4. Toads use their back legs for jumping. _____

5. Toads lay their eggs on land. _____

6. Toads have a poison in their skin. _____

7. Snakes are food for toads. _____

B. Draw lines to complete the sentences.

1. Toads lay their eggs   rain puddles.

2. A desert toad leaves its hole when   in water.

3. Raccoons roll toads on the ground   it rains.

4. The tadpoles of desert toads live in   rough and dry.

5. A toad has a skin that is   to get rid of the poison on their skin.

C. Write frog, toad, or both to answer the questions.

1. Which amphibian has longer back legs? _____

2. Which amphibian has dry, bumpy skin? _____

3. Which amphibian has young called tadpoles? _____

4. Which amphibian spends more time on land? _____

5. Which amphibian has a long, sticky tongue? _____

6. Which amphibian eats insects for food? _____

7. Which amphibian has a poison in its skin? _____

8. Which amphibian makes croaking sounds? _____

9. Which amphibian lays eggs in water? _____

45

Salamanders

Yellow-Spotted Salamander

Salamanders look very different from frogs and toads. They have very short legs. They move by walking. When they hatch, young salamanders have legs. Adults have a long tail.

Salamanders are like frogs and toads in some ways. Salamanders are cold-blooded. They have moist skin. They eat worms and insects.

Salamanders lay eggs in the water. The young have gills and spend the first stage of their lives in the water. Most adult salamanders grow lungs and live on land. Salamanders are found under rocks and logs in cool, damp places.

The giant salamander of Japan is 5 feet long. But most salamanders are less than 6 inches long.

A. **Answer <u>True</u> or <u>False</u>.**

1. Salamanders are cold-blooded. _____

2. Young salamanders have lungs. _____

3. An adult salamander has a long tail. _____

B. **Answer the questions.**

1. Where do salamanders lay their eggs? _____

2. What do salamanders eat? _____

_____

46

Part A

Read each sentence. Write <u>True</u> if the sentence is true and <u>False</u> if it is false.

1. Amphibians are cold-blooded animals. _____

2. Young frogs are called salamanders. _____

3. Amphibians and insects are invertebrates. _____

4. Gills help a tadpole breathe in water. _____

5. The poison on a toad's skin can harm a person. _____

6. Desert toads lay their eggs in rain puddles. _____

7. Frogs have webbed feet that help them swim. _____

8. Salamanders lose their tails when they become adults. _____

Part B

On each blank, write the word that completes the sentence. Use the words below.

amphibians	lungs	toad
frog	salamander	vertebrate
gills	tadpole	

1. An animal with a backbone is called a _____.

2. Frogs, toads, and salamanders are all _____.

3. An adult amphibian with a tail is a _____.

4. Most adult amphibians breathe with _____.

5. An amphibian with dry, bumpy skin is a _____.

6. A young frog is called a _____.

7. Young amphibians breathe with _____.

Make a Model Frog

You Need

- frog pattern
- tagboard
- scissors
- 5 push-through fasteners
- crayons or paints

1. Make a model of a frog. Copy the frog pattern from the blackline master onto tagboard. Cut out the pieces.

2. Assemble the frog model. Put *A1* on top of *A*, *B1* on top of *B*, and so on. Use push-through fasteners to put the parts of the frog together. Then color or paint your frog.

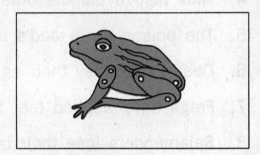

3. A frog's short front legs help it sit up. Show how a frog sits, as in the top picture.

4. A frog's strong hind legs help it jump. Most frogs can jump 20 times their own length. Show how a frog jumps, as in the second picture.

5. A frog's hind legs also help it swim. Show how a frog swims, as in the third picture.

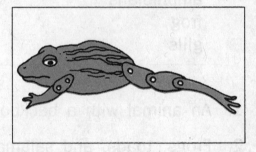

Write the Answer

How are a frog's long, powerful hind legs a good adaptation for an amphibian?

_____

_____

_____

Fill in the circle in front of the word or phrase that best completes each sentence. The first one is done for you.

1. All amphibians
   - ⓐ walk.
   - ⬤ lay eggs.
   - ⓒ have dry skin.

2. Toads that live in the desert
   - ⓐ have gills.
   - ⓑ live in trees.
   - ⓒ live in holes until it rains.

3. Most amphibians lay their eggs
   - ⓐ in a nest.
   - ⓑ in water.
   - ⓒ under a rock.

4. To get air through their skin, amphibians must
   - ⓐ stay moist.
   - ⓑ eat insects.
   - ⓒ live in holes.

5. Young frogs and toads are called
   - ⓐ salamanders.
   - ⓑ insects.
   - ⓒ tadpoles.

6. Frogs and toads both have
   - ⓐ smooth skin.
   - ⓑ long, sticky tongues.
   - ⓒ long tails.

Fill in the missing words.

7. All vertebrates have a _____. (tail, backbone)

8. A tadpole breathes with _____. (gills, lungs)

9. Most amphibians feed on _____.
   (plants, insects)

Write the answer on the lines.

10. Amphibians are cold-blooded animals. What happens to them as the outside temperature changes?

_____

_____

UNIT 4
Reptiles

What Is a Reptile?

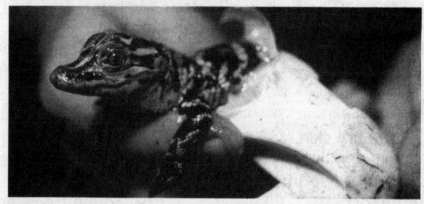

Alligators Hatching

What do turtles, alligators, crocodiles, snakes, and lizards have in common? They are all **reptiles**. Reptiles are vertebrates. Vertebrates are animals with backbones. You have already learned about amphibians, another group of vertebrate animals.

Snakes and a few lizards do not have legs. Most other reptiles have four legs. The end of each leg has five toes with claws. A reptile's skin is dry, thick, and waterproof. The skin is covered with **scales** or hard plates. Some reptiles, like snakes, must **shed** their skins in order to grow.

A reptile is cold-blooded. Remember that being cold-blooded means that an animal is as warm or as cold as the temperature around it. Reptiles live in warm places. If the weather is very hot during the day, reptiles rest. Then they are active at night when it is cool.

A reptile breathes air with its lungs, as you do. The air mixes with blood in its lungs. The reptile's heart moves the blood around the body.

Most reptiles reproduce by laying eggs on land. Many lay eggs with tough, leathery shells. Others have eggs with hard shells. The young of some reptiles do not hatch from eggs but are born alive. Most young reptiles care for themselves as soon as they are born. But some reptiles protect their young for up to 12 weeks.

A. Answer True or False.

1. A snake is a kind of reptile. _____

2. Reptiles are invertebrate animals. _____

3. Most reptiles lay eggs on land. _____

4. Reptiles have gills instead of lungs. _____

5. Some reptiles are born alive. _____

B. Write the letter for the correct answer.

1. All of these animals are reptiles except _____.
   (a) turtles   (b) alligators   (c) cows

2. Reptiles have skin covered with _____.
   (a) scales   (b) feathers   (c) hair

3. The body temperature of a reptile is always _____.
   (a) cold   (b) hot   (c) the same as the temperature around it

C. Answer the questions.

1. How are reptiles and amphibians alike? _____

   _____

   _____

2. Why do some reptiles shed their skins? _____

   _____

3. What kinds of reptiles do not have legs? _____

   _____

4. How do most reptiles reproduce? _____

   _____

5. When do most young reptiles begin to care for themselves? _____

   _____

   _____

Turtles

Box Turtle

Turtles Hatching

A **turtle** is the only reptile with a shell. The shell is made of hard, bony plates. It is round on top and flat on the bottom. The shell keeps the turtle safe. When a turtle is in danger, it can pull in its head, legs, and tail. No enemy can get in.

Most turtles live in water. A few kinds live both on land and in water. A **tortoise** is a turtle that lives only on land. Tortoises and box turtles are the only kinds of turtles that live just on land.

Tortoises like dry places. Gopher tortoises dig holes in sandy soil. They make these holes their homes. They may even share them with other animals.

Box turtles live in moist woods and fields. They feed mainly on plants. But they will also eat insects and earthworms. Box turtles hibernate in cold winters and lay their eggs in the summer.

Turtles do not have teeth. A turtle uses its sharp, hard beak to break food into pieces. Many turtles eat both plants and animals. Most tortoises eat only plants.

Turtles that live in the water can grow to be very large, but most land turtles are less than 8 inches long. Tortoises can grow to be 14 inches long.

Scientists believe that turtles live longer than any other vertebrate animal. Some tortoises and box turtles have lived for more than 100 years.

A female land turtle lays 3 to 5 eggs at one time. She buries them in the ground and goes away. The young can take care of themselves as soon as they are born.

A. Write the letter for the correct answer.

1. A turtle protects itself by _____.
   (a) running (b) hitting (c) pulling inside its shell

2. A tortoise lives _____.
   (a) on land and in water (b) on land (c) in water

3. In the hole that a gopher tortoise digs, you may find _____.
   (a) sticks (b) water (c) other animals

4. After laying and burying eggs, a female turtle _____.
   (a) goes away (b) puts water on them (c) sits on them

B. Answer the questions.

1. Since a turtle does not have teeth, how does it eat its food? _____
   _____

2. Are young turtles cared for by their parents? Explain why or why not.
   _____
   _____
   _____

3. How does its shell keep a turtle safe? _____
   _____
   _____

4. Which kinds of turtles live just on land? _____
   _____

C. Use each word to write a sentence about turtles.

1. tortoise _____
   _____

2. eggs _____
   _____

Crocodiles

Alligator

Crocodile

How is a crocodile's snout different from an alligator's snout?

When do you think **crocodiles** first appeared on Earth? More than 150 million years ago! In all that time, crocodiles have not changed much.

Crocodiles have long, flat bodies that are covered with a tough skin. They have four short legs and a long, powerful tail.

Crocodiles live in many different countries. In the United States, they live in salty water along the Florida coast.

Thousands of crocodiles used to live there. But many of them were killed for their skins. By 1975, less than 20 crocodile nests were counted.

Then the crocodile was put on the list of endangered animals. These animals are now protected by laws. They cannot be hunted. In 1987, 29 nests were counted. Although they are still endangered, crocodiles in Florida are increasing in number.

Crocodiles and alligators are about the same shape and size. The usual length of an adult American crocodile is 12 feet, slightly longer than an alligator. A crocodile's snout is more pointed than an alligator's snout. When an alligator shuts its jaw, its teeth cannot be seen. But when a crocodile shuts its mouth, you can see its teeth.

Female crocodiles lay between 20 and 50 eggs. They make nests for the eggs or bury them in sand. As the young start to hatch, they make sounds. When the female hears the sounds, she helps dig the young crocodiles out.

A. **Write the letter for the correct answer.**

1. Crocodiles first appeared on Earth _____ .
   (a) 50 years ago   (b) 5,000 years ago   (c) 150 million years ago

2. Since crocodiles are on the endangered animals list, they cannot be _____ .
   (a) hunted   (b) photographed   (c) seen

3. You can tell a crocodile from an alligator by the shape of its _____ .
   (a) tail   (b) legs   (c) snout

B. **Use each word to write a sentence about crocodiles.**

1. endangered _____

_____

2. snout _____

_____

C. **Answer True or False.**

1. Crocodiles live in salty water. _____

2. People used to kill crocodiles for their skins. _____

3. Crocodiles have never been endangered. _____

D. **Answer the questions.**

1. How does a female crocodile know when her eggs are beginning to hatch? _____

_____

2. If you saw a crocodile and an alligator, both with their mouths closed, how could you tell which was which? _____

_____

_____

Alligators

Alligators can be found in the southeastern United States. They swim in lakes, rivers, or swamps. Alligators eat fish, birds, and frogs. These animals are their **prey**.

The alligator has a large head. Its snout is not as pointed as a crocodile's snout. The alligator's eyes and nostrils are above water when the alligator swims. That way, alligators can see and breathe easily. But their prey may not see them. Then the alligators grab their prey with their strong jaws.

An alligator may grow to almost 12 feet in length. It can weigh up to 550 pounds. Its body is covered with thick, hard scales.

In winter, the alligator hibernates. It may dig a wide, deep hole and stay there during the winter months.

Adult male alligators often roar. At mating time, these loud sounds may help the male and female find each other. After mating, the female builds a nest with grasses and twigs near the water. Then she lays between 20 and 70 eggs and covers them. After 9 to 10 weeks, the eggs begin to hatch.

Like crocodiles, the young alligators make noise. The female hears the noise and helps the young dig out of their nest. The female may take care of the young for a few weeks.

A. Use each word to write a sentence about alligators.

1. crocodiles _____

_____

2. prey _____

_____

3. hibernates _____

_____

4. nostrils _____

_____

B. Fill in the missing words.

1. An alligator's snout is not as _____ as a crocodile's snout. (rounded, pointed)

2. Alligators can breathe easily when they swim because their

_____ stick out of the water. (tails, nostrils)

3. An alligator eats frogs, birds, and _____. (fish, crocodiles)

4. The female alligator builds a nest of grasses and twigs near the

_____. (rocks, water)

C. Answer <u>True</u> or <u>False</u>.

1. An alligator may grow to almost 12 feet in length. _____

2. Alligators do not make sounds. _____

3. The female alligator builds a nest for its eggs. _____

4. An alligator may dig a hole and hibernate during the winter.

_____

5. When young alligators begin to hatch, they make noises. _____

6. The female alligator lays only one egg. _____

7. Female alligators never take care of their young. _____

Snakes

Common Snakes

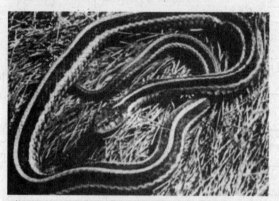

Garter Snake

Racer Snake

Do you think **snakes** are slimy? They are not. Snakes are covered with dry, tough scales. Snakes do not have legs. Yet they can move along the ground. Some can swim. Others can even climb trees!

All snakes are carnivores. With their special jaws, snakes can open their mouths very wide. This lets a snake swallow a whole animal that is twice as large as the snake's head. The animal is broken down by chemicals in a snake's body.

As a snake grows, it sheds its skin. This happens 3 to 6 times a year.

Two common snakes are garter snakes and racers. Both kinds are found all over the United States.

Garter snakes grow to be about 2 feet long. They have 3 light stripes that run along their body. Garter snakes do not lay eggs. The young are born alive. Garter snakes eat frogs, fish, mice, and birds. Garter snakes are **nonpoisonous**. Their bite has no poison.

Racers are about 4 feet long. They can be dark green, blue, or black. The young hatch from eggs. Racers climb well and move fast. Racers hunt for food in the day. They eat insects, lizards, and other snakes. They also eat frogs, mice, and birds. If you try to catch a racer, it may bite you. But, like garter snakes, racers are nonpoisonous.

A. Answer True or False.

1. Most snakes have four legs. _____

2. A snake sheds its skin only once in its life. _____

3. Snakes cannot swim or climb trees. _____

4. Garter snakes are born alive. _____

5. Racers hunt at night. _____

B. Use the words below to complete the sentences.

carnivores	jaws	racers
eggs	poison	scales

1. With their special _____, snakes can open their mouths very wide.

2. All snakes eat other animals. Snakes are _____.

3. Two common kinds of snakes are garter snakes and _____.

4. Snakes are covered with dry, tough _____.

5. A bite from a garter snake has no _____.

C. Answer the questions.

1. What happens to a snake's skin as the snake grows? _____

_____

2. Where can snakes move? _____

_____

_____

3. Why is a snake's jaw special? _____

_____

_____

_____

Snakes
Large Snakes

After a meal like this, a constrictor may not eat again for more than a year.

Some of the largest snakes in the world are **constrictors**. They wrap themselves around an animal so it cannot breathe. Once the animal is dead, the snake swallows it whole. Remember that a snake's jaw allows it to swallow big animals. Large constrictors can swallow an animal that weighs 100 pounds. One constrictor swallowed a leopard! After such a meal, many large snakes do not eat again for more than a year.

The largest constrictors are members of the boa family. Although some boas are small, three are very large. They are the anaconda, the python, and the boa constrictor.

Anacondas live in swamps and rivers in South America. Anacondas often grow to be about 25 feet long. One anaconda was found that was more than 37 feet long.

When a python hatches, it is about 2 feet long. Pythons grow about 2 feet a year. The largest python ever seen was 33 feet long. Pythons are found in Africa and Asia.

The boa constrictor is next in size. Boa constrictors live in South America. They hang from trees and attack animals that pass under them. Unlike anacondas and pythons, these snakes do not lay eggs. Their young are born alive. A female may give birth to 50 snakes at one time.

A. **Write the letter for the correct answer.**

1. Some of the largest snakes in the world are _____.
   (a) racers   (b) constrictors   (c) garter snakes

2. Constrictors wrap themselves around an animal so it _____.
   (a) can see   (b) cannot breathe   (c) cannot hear

3. Although some boas are small, three are _____.
   (a) even smaller   (b) very large   (c) medium-size

4. After eating, many large snakes do not eat again for _____.
   (a) a day   (b) a week   (c) more than a year

5. One anaconda was found that was more than _____ long.
   (a) 37 inches   (b) 37 feet   (c) 370 feet

B. **Use each word to write a sentence about large snakes.**

1. constrictors _____

   _____

2. anaconda _____

   _____

3. python _____

   _____

C. **Use the words below to complete the sentences.**

anacondas	hatches	racer
boa constrictor	largest	

1. Some of the _____ snakes in the world are constrictors.

2. When a python _____, it is about 2 feet long.

3. A snake that does not lay eggs is the _____.

4. Snakes that live in swamps and rivers in South America are

   _____.

Snakes

Poisonous Snakes

Rattlesnake

Water Moccasin

There are about 300 kinds of **poisonous** snakes in the world. A person can get sick or die from the bite of these snakes.

Scientists group poisonous snakes by the way that they bite. One group of snakes has long **fangs**. Rattlesnakes and cottonmouths are in this group. When the snake bites, a poison called **venom** goes through the fangs.

In the United States, rattlesnakes bite more people than any other kind of snake. Before it bites, a rattlesnake may shake its tail to warn its enemies to stay away. The noise its tail makes sounds like a rattle.

Cottonmouths are usually found in the southeastern United States. When a cottonmouth is angry, it shows the white inside of its mouth, which looks like cotton. These snakes are also called water moccasins. But they do not always stay in the water.

The other group of poisonous snakes have shorter fangs than a rattlesnake. These snakes do not just bite. They hang on and chew. Coral snakes belong to this group. These brightly colored snakes can be found from the southern United States to South America. They can grow to about 4 feet long.

The cobra belongs to the same group as the coral snake. The king cobra, which lives in parts of Asia, is the largest poisonous snake in the world. It can grow to be 18 feet long.

A. Answer the questions.

1. How do scientists group poisonous snakes? _____

_____

2. Which snake bites more people in the United States than any

other snake? _____

_____

3. Why does a rattlesnake shake its tail? _____

_____

4. How do you think the cottonmouth got its name? _____

_____

B. Answer True or False.

1. A person cannot die from the bite of a poisonous snake. _____

2. The poison in a snake's fangs is called venom. _____

3. Rattlesnakes never bite people. _____

4. Cottonmouths open their mouth to show they are happy. _____

5. The water moccasin does not always stay in the water. _____

6. The coral snake bites the same way as the rattlesnake. _____

7. The largest poisonous snake is the king cobra. _____

C. Use each word to write a sentence about poisonous snakes.

1. rattlesnake _____

_____

2. fangs _____

_____

3. cottonmouth _____

_____

Lizards

Desert Iguana

Gecko

Most **lizards** have dry, scaly skin, four legs, and a tail. Some lizards do not have legs and look like snakes. Large lizards look like crocodiles. The smallest lizard is about 3 inches long. The largest lizard, the Komono dragon, can grow to be 10 feet long.

Because they are cold-blooded, most lizards live in warm places. Lizards are the most common reptiles found in deserts. Lizards live on the ground or in trees. Some lizards have special sticky toes. A gecko is a lizard that can walk upside down on a ceiling!

A few lizards eat plants instead of animals. But most lizards eat insects and other small animals. The Komono dragon can eat small deer and wild pigs.

Most lizards hatch from eggs. Some kinds of lizards are born alive. Young lizards can take care of themselves as soon as they are born.

A. Write the letter for the correct answer.

1. Which of the following is not a lizard? _____
   (a) Komono dragon　　(b) gecko　　(c) cottonmouth

2. Where would you find lizards living? _____
   (a) oceans　　(b) warm places　　(c) cold places

3. What do most lizards eat? _____
   (a) leaves　　(b) crocodiles　　(c) insects

B. Answer True or False.

1. Most lizards have two legs and wet, slimy skin. _____

2. Most lizards hatch from eggs. _____

Part A

Read each sentence. Write <u>True</u> if the sentence is true. Write <u>False</u> if the sentence is false.

1. Most reptiles reproduce by laying eggs. _____

2. Because reptiles are cold-blooded, they live in cold places. _____

3. Lizards have dry, scaly skin. _____

4. Turtles have many sharp teeth to eat their food. _____

5. When garter snakes bite, venom goes through their fangs. _____

6. The alligator's snout is exactly like the crocodile's. _____

7. After burying its eggs, the female turtle goes away. _____

8. The king cobra is the only kind of snake that has legs. _____

Part B

Use the words below to complete the sentences.

animals	crocodile	reptiles
boa	lizards	turtle
cold-blooded	python	

1. Snakes can open their mouths wide to swallow large _____.

2. An animal on the list of endangered animals is the _____.

3. The only reptile with a shell is the _____.

4. Turtles, alligators, snakes, and lizards are all _____.

5. An animal that is as warm or cold as the temperature around it is

   _____ .

6. The most common reptiles found in the desert are _____.

7. The largest constrictors are members of the _____ family.

EXPLORE & DISCOVER

Make a Snake Skin

You Need

- color pictures of snakes
- tagboard
- markers or paints
- wax paper
- scissors
- clear tape

1. Look at the pictures of snakes. Notice that most of them have beautiful color patterns. The color comes from a deep layer of the snake's skin.

2. Draw a snake on tagboard. Use markers or paints to make a color pattern on your snake. Cut the snake out.

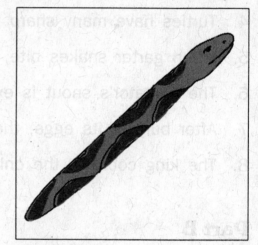

3. The top layer of a snake's skin is made of tough scales. Make scales for your snake out of wax paper. Cut a piece of wax paper the same length as your snake and twice as wide. Draw scales on the wax paper with a pencil.

4. Fold the wax paper loosely around your snake and tape it together as shown in the picture. Do <u>not</u> tape the wax paper to the snake.

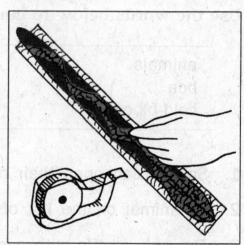

5. As a snake grows it sheds its skin. Slide the wax paper off your snake to have the snake shed its top layer of skin.

Write the Answer

How does a snake's skin protect it?

_____

_____

_____

Fill in the circle in front of the word or phrase that best completes each sentence. The first one is done for you.

1. A cold-blooded animal is
   - ⓐ always cold.
   - ⓑ always warm.
   - ● as warm or as cold as the temperature around it.

2. A reptile on the list of endangered animals is the
   - ⓐ coral snake.
   - ⓑ crocodile.
   - ⓒ boa.

3. The most common reptile found in the desert is the
   - ⓐ lizard.
   - ⓑ crocodile.
   - ⓒ turtle.

4. The poisonous snake that bites more people in the United States than any other snake is the
   - ⓐ anaconda.
   - ⓑ racer.
   - ⓒ rattlesnake.

5. A turtle protects itself by
   - ⓐ closing its eyes.
   - ⓑ making a bad smell.
   - ⓒ pulling inside its shell.

6. Snakes are covered with
   - ⓐ hard shells.
   - ⓑ dry scales.
   - ⓒ slimy skin.

Fill in the missing words.

7. A reptile without legs is the _____.
   (snake, turtle)

8. All snakes are _____. (omnivores, carnivores)

9. Reptiles breathe with _____. (gills, lungs)

Write the answer on the lines.

10. How do most reptiles reproduce?

_____

_____

UNIT 5
Birds

Ostrich

Robin

What Is a Bird?

Birds are like amphibians and reptiles in some ways. Birds, amphibians, and reptiles are all vertebrates. They have backbones. Like amphibians and most reptiles, birds reproduce by laying eggs All three groups of animals breathe with lungs. Yet birds are different from amphibians and reptiles in some ways.

Birds are **warm-blooded.** The body temperature of a warm-blooded animal always stays the same. Remember that the body temperature of a cold-blooded animal changes as the temperature around it changes.

Birds have feathers and wings. Feathers help birds stay warm and dry. Both wings and feathers help birds fly. But not all birds can fly.

Most birds make nests for homes. Nests can be made of twigs or mud. Others are holes in trees. The female lays eggs in the nest. The young that hatch stay in the nest until they are strong enough to fly.

Many birds live in groups, or **flocks**. Many flocks of birds that live in the north migrate to warmer areas in the south during the winter. They travel south to find food. Then they return north to nest in the spring.

There are over 8,600 kinds of birds. The largest bird is the ostrich. It is more than 8 feet tall and can weigh 300 pounds. The smallest bird is the hummingbird. One kind of hummingbird is less than 3 inches long.

A. Answer True or False.

1. Birds are cold-blooded animals. _____

2. Birds have backbones. _____

3. Birds have feathers on their bodies. _____

4. Birds reproduce by laying eggs. _____

5. Birds use their wings to fly. _____

6. All birds can fly. _____

7. Many birds make nests. _____

8. Birds breathe with their gills. _____

B. Write the letter for the correct answer.

1. Which animals lay eggs? _____
   (a) amphibians   (b) reptiles   (c) birds   (d) a, b, and c

2. Which animals are warm-blooded? _____
   (a) reptiles   (b) amphibians   (c) birds

3. Which animals have feathers and wings? _____
   (a) birds   (b) amphibians   (c) reptiles

4. Which animals can fly? _____
   (a) reptiles   (b) birds   (c) amphibians

C. Answer the questions.

1. In what three ways are birds different from reptiles and amphibians?

   _____

   _____

2. What is a group of birds called? _____

   _____

3. What does being warm-blooded mean? _____

   _____

   _____

Penguins

Emperor Penguins

You might not know that a penguin is a bird. Penguins stand up on short legs and waddle or hop when they walk. Penguins cannot fly. Instead, they use their wings to help them swim. They also have webbed feet for swimming. Penguins spend much of their time in the water looking for fish to eat.

Penguins come in many sizes. The smallest penguin is about 1 foot tall. The largest is the emperor penguin. It can be 4 feet tall.

Penguins live in the southern half of the world. They are found only in places where the ocean water is very cold. Some, for example, live in Antarctica.

Penguins are black and white and have a thick layer of feathers. The feathers are waterproof. So even when a penguin swims, the cold water does not reach its skin. A penguin also has a layer of fat under its skin that acts like a blanket to keep it warm.

Penguins lay eggs, but they do not build nests. Most penguins lay their eggs on the ground or in holes.

Emperor penguins spend most of their time on the ice. If an emperor penguin left its egg on the ice, the egg would freeze. So as soon as the female lays an egg, the male rolls it onto his feet. He keeps the egg warm. The male does not eat for 2 months. During this time, the female eats fish in the ocean. When the egg hatches, the female comes back to take care of the young. Then the male penguin goes off to feed.

A. Answer <u>True</u> or <u>False</u>.

1. Penguins use their wings to fly. _____

2. Penguins live in warm ocean water. _____

3. Penguins eat fish for food. _____

4. Penguin feathers are waterproof. _____

B. Choose the phrases that describe penguins. Write them on the lines.

_____

can fly	lay eggs	thick layer of feathers
eat fruit	layer of fat	webbed feet
have wings	swim well	

_____

1. _____

2. _____

3. _____

4. _____

5. _____

6. _____

C. Answer the questions.

1. What do penguins use to help them swim? _____

_____

_____

2. How does a penguin keep warm? _____

_____

_____

3. Why does a male emperor penguin keep an egg on his feet? _____

_____

_____

Pelicans

White Pelican

Brown Pelican

Pelicans are large birds. They can be 5 feet long and their wings can spread out to 10 feet. These huge wings help pelicans to fly very high and stay in the air for hours. Pelicans are also good swimmers. Their webbed feet help pelicans move easily through the water.

There are 6 kinds of pelicans. The white pelican and the brown pelican live in North America. The brown pelican is found along coastlines. The white pelican lives mainly near large lakes.

Pelicans live in large groups called **colonies**. They build their nests on the ground or in trees along the shore. Sometimes there are hundreds of nests in one colony.

Pelicans have large pouches of skin beneath their beaks. These pouches can hold 3 gallons of water. Pelicans use their pouches to catch the fish they use for food.

Pelicans catch fish in different ways. When a white pelican sees a fish from the air, it lands on the surface of the water with a splash. Then it dips its head underwater and scoops up the fish with its pouch. When a brown pelican sees fish, it dives into the water at a great speed. Then it grabs as many fish as it can before it floats back to the surface.

A. Answer the questions.

1. What helps a pelican swim? _____

_____

2. What does a pelican use to catch fish? _____

_____

3. How does a white pelican catch its food? _____

_____

_____

4. How does a brown pelican catch its food? _____

_____

_____

B. Write <u>pelican</u>, <u>penguin</u>, or <u>both</u> to answer the questions.

1. Which bird has webbed feet? _____

2. Which bird has wings? _____

3. Which bird can fly? _____

4. Which bird eats fish? _____

5. Which bird catches fish in its pouch? _____

6. Which bird lives only where the ocean water is cold? _____

7. Which bird can swim? _____

C. Write the word or words that best finish each sentence.

1. Pelicans can be found living near oceans and large _____.

2. Pelicans nest in big groups called _____.

3. A pelican catches food in its _____.

4. Pelicans eat _____.

5. Pelicans build nests in trees or on the _____.

Ducks and Geese

Male

Female

Mallard Ducks

Canada Geese

Ducks and geese are called waterfowl. Ducks and geese can be found in almost every lake in the world. Ducks are smaller than geese. They have shorter necks than geese. A duck quacks. A goose honks.

Ducks and geese spend much of their time in the water. They have many adaptations for living in water. Both ducks and geese have webbed feet. Webbed feet help ducks and geese swim. They move like paddles to push the birds through the water.

Ducks and geese also have special feathers. Their feathers are coated with oil so the birds stay dry even when they are in water. Young ducks and geese have feathers called **down.** Down is very soft and thick. It helps to keep the young birds warm. Adult ducks and geese have a layer of down under their feathers.

Ducks and geese build their nests on the ground. They line their nests with their soft down feathers. Young ducks and geese can swim soon after they hatch. They can also feed themselves. They stay with their mothers for safety until they can fly.

Ducks and geese that nest in the north migrate in the winter. They fly south to find warmer weather and food.

Many ducks and geese eat plants that grow underwater. To reach the plants, they first tip upside down with their heads in the water. Then they stretch their long necks to reach the plants. They use their flat beaks to pull up the plants and then they turn rightside up again.

A. Answer the questions.

1. What are ducks and geese called? _____

_____

2. What are the soft feathers of ducks and geese called? _____

_____

3. What are the feathers of adult ducks and geese coated with?

_____

4. Why do ducks and geese fly south in the winter? _____

_____

B. Write <u>duck</u>, <u>goose</u>, or <u>both</u> to answer the questions.

1. Which bird can swim? _____

2. Which bird makes a quacking sound? _____

3. Which bird makes a honking sound? _____

4. Which bird has down? _____

5. Which bird is larger? _____

6. Which bird has webbed feet? _____

7. Which bird migrates? _____

8. Which bird is a waterfowl? _____

C. Answer <u>True</u> or <u>False</u>.

1. A goose has a long neck. _____

2. Ducks and geese use their flat beaks to pull up underwater plants.

_____

3. Ducks and geese build nests in trees. _____

4. Young ducks and geese can swim soon after they hatch. _____

5. Down feathers help keep young birds warm. _____

Eagles and Hawks

Bald Eagle

Red-Tailed Hawk

Eagles and hawks are carnivorous birds. They eat other animals. They both have long, sharp claws called **talons** to grab and hold their food. Eagles and hawks also have sharp, curved beaks for cutting and tearing meat.

Eagles and hawks are very good fliers. They spend much of their time **soaring** in the air. Soaring is flying without flapping the wings. Eagles and hawks can soar for hours.

Eagles and hawks have good eyesight. They can spot a mouse while they are flying hundreds of feet above the ground.

Hawks are smaller than eagles, and they eat smaller animals. Some small hawks eat insects, snakes, or frogs. The red-tailed hawk can find food while soaring in the air. Then it dives toward the ground at about 120 miles an hour. The red-tailed hawk eats mice, snakes, birds, and other small animals.

Some eagles catch and eat fish. A few eagles are so big that they can catch monkeys and small deer. Many eagles and hawks eat mice and rabbits. Mice and rabbits can damage farm crops. Although eagles and hawks help farmers by eating mice and rabbits, some people shoot these birds. There are now laws against shooting eagles and hawks.

Eagles and hawks build very big nests. Some can be 6 feet wide and 3 feet deep. Some eagles and hawks build their nests in trees. Others nest on cliffs or on the ground.

A. Answer True or False.

1. Hawks and eagles eat mostly plants. _____

2. Hawks and eagles grab their food with their claws. _____

3. A hawk's beak can cut and tear meat. _____

4. Eagles are smaller than hawks. _____

5. All eagles and hawks eat the same animal foods. _____

6. Carnivorous birds eat other animals. _____

7. Hawks and eagles have sharp, curved beaks. _____

B. Choose the word that best matches the description.

beaks	monkeys	soaring
eagles	rabbits	talons

1. These are sharp claws for grabbing food. _____

2. This is flying without flapping wings. _____

3. Eagles and hawks use these for cutting meat. _____

4. A few eagles are so big they can eat these. _____

5. Hawks and eagles help farmers by eating these. _____

6. These are bigger than hawks. _____

C. Draw lines to complete the sentences.

1. Hawks use talons to   on cliffs.

2. Hawks are smaller than   eyesight.

3. Some eagles and hawks nest   grab their food.

4. Eagles and hawks have good   eagles.

5. There are laws against shooting   eagles and hawks.

77

Chickens and Turkeys

Domestic Chickens

Male Turkey

Chickens and turkeys are **domestic animals,** animals that have been tamed by people. People raise chickens and turkeys for their meat. Chickens are also raised for their eggs. Most chickens usually lay more than 240 eggs a year.

Wild turkeys can still be found in many parts of the United States. Wild chickens live in the forests of Asia. Both wild and domestic chickens and turkeys can fly only a few yards at a time.

A male chicken is called a rooster. A female chicken is called a hen. Both have fleshy red pieces of skin on their head. The skin on top of a chicken's head is called a comb. The skin under the beak is called a wattle. Males have bigger combs and wattles than females.

Turkeys are larger than chickens. Male turkeys are called toms. Female turkeys are called hens. Females are smaller and not as colorful as males. Male turkeys have long wattles, but no comb. Instead, they have a long piece of skin called a snood that hangs over their beak.

Wild turkeys live in small flocks in the forest. They walk on the ground and look for seeds, fruit, and insects to eat. At night, turkeys sleep in trees. Wild turkeys lay their eggs on the ground in a nest made of leaves.

Male turkeys have a special display to attract females. A male puffs up his feathers until he is almost round. Then he spreads his colorful tail like a fan and dances in a circle.

A. Use the words below to answer the questions.

chicken	domestic	rooster	turkey
comb	hen	tom	wattle

1. What is an animal that is tamed by people called? _____

2. What is a male turkey called? _____

3. What is the skin on top of a chicken's head called? _____

4. Which bird is raised for its eggs? _____

5. What is the skin under a chicken's beak called? _____

6. What is a female turkey called? _____

7. What is a male chicken called? _____

8. Which bird is larger? _____

B. Write chicken, turkey, or both to answer the questions.

1. Which bird is a domestic animal? _____

2. Which bird can fly only a few yards? _____

3. Which bird has a comb? _____

4. Which bird is found wild in the United States? _____

5. Which bird has a special display to attract females? _____

6. Which bird is raised for its meat? _____

C. Answer the questions.

1. Where do wild turkeys lay their eggs? _____

_____

2. Why do people raise chickens and turkeys? _____

_____

_____

Parrots

Parrot

Parakeet

Have you heard of birds that can talk? A talking bird is probably a parrot. A parrot can be taught to say words. When a parrot talks, it doesn't understand what it is saying. It only repeats the sounds that it hears.

There are more than 300 kinds of parrots. Some are only a few inches long. Others can be over 3 feet long. Many are very colorful. Parrots may be red, blue, green, or yellow. Many parrots are more than one color.

Most parrots live in tropical forests or jungles. They live, travel, and feed in groups called flocks. Most parrots nest in holes in trees.

Parrots eat fruit and seeds. They have strong, sharp beaks to help them pick fruit and break open seeds. Parrots are also one of the few birds that use their feet to hold food. They pick up food with their claws and lift it to their beaks.

Wild parrots are very loud. A flock of parrots can be heard for miles. Parrots do not sing like other birds. They chatter or screech.

Many kinds of parrots are kept as pets. Parakeets are small parrots that are often kept as pets. Large parrots are better at learning to talk than small parrots.

Many wild parrots were once caught and sold for pets. They were becoming rare. But now there are laws to protect wild parrots. Most parrots that are sold today come from people that breed their own pet parrots.

A. Answer True or False.

1. Parrots understand words. _____

2. Parrots eat mice and fish. _____

3. Wild parrots are protected by law. _____

4. Parrots are good singers. _____

5. Parrots have strong, sharp beaks. _____

6. Wild parrots live in flocks. _____

7. Parrots are kept as pets. _____

B. Draw lines to complete the sentences.

1. Parrots nest in   protect wild parrots.

2. Parrots eat   to hold food.

3. There are laws to   the parakeet.

4. Parrots use their feet   holes in trees.

5. One kind of small parrot is   fruit and seeds.

6. Wild parrots live in   tropical forests.

C. Answer the questions.

1. How many different kinds of parrots are there? _____

_____

2. Where do wild parrots live? _____

_____

3. What do parrots eat? _____

4. How does a parrot "talk"? _____

_____

5. Why were wild parrots becoming rare? _____

_____

81

Owls

Screech Owl

Burrowing Owl

Most birds are active during the day and sleep during the night. A few kinds of birds are active at night and sleep during the day. Owls are probably the best-known birds that are active at night.

You can recognize an owl by its short, thick body and broad head. Unlike other birds, owls have eyes that point straight ahead. Owls can't move their eyes like you can. So they have to turn their heads to see moving objects.

Like hawks and eagles, owls are carnivores. Owls eat the same kinds of food, but they hunt at night. Like hawks and eagles, owls have sharp talons for grabbing animals. They also have sharp, curved beaks for cutting and tearing meat. Owls can swallow small animals whole.

Owls have special feathers that help them fly silently. Silent flight helps them sneak up on animals they are hunting.

Because they hunt in the dark, owls need good hearing to find their food. An owl can hear a mouse move in the forest. Then it can fly down and grab the mouse without ever seeing it. But owls also have sharp eyesight. They can see much better in darkness than people can.

Owls nest in many different places. Some large owls use empty hawk or eagle nests. The burrowing owl lives on the plains, where there are few trees. It nests in holes dug by prairie dogs or other animals. The snowy owl lives in the Arctic tundra, where there are no tall trees. It nests on the snowy ground.

A. Use the words below to complete the sentences.

| carnivores | feathers | night |
| eyesight | nests | talons |

1. Special _____ help owls fly silently.

2. Like hawks and eagles, owls are _____.

3. Owls grab animals with their _____.

4. Owls are active at _____.

5. With their sharp _____, owls can see better in darkness than people can.

B. Answer <u>True</u> or <u>False</u>.

1. Owls are active during the day. _____

2. Owls can swallow small animals whole. _____

3. Owls do not have good eyesight. _____

4. Owls can fly silently. _____

5. Owls have good hearing. _____

6. Owls have to turn their heads to see moving objects. _____

7. Owls eat only plants. _____

8. All owls nest in the same kinds of places. _____

C. Write <u>owl</u>, <u>hawk</u>, or <u>both</u> to answer the questions.

1. Which bird can see well at night? _____

2. Which bird hunts for animals during the day? _____

3. Which bird has a sharp beak? _____

4. Which bird has special feathers that help it fly silently? _____

5. Which bird uses its hearing to catch animals? _____

6. Which bird has eyes that point straight ahead? _____

Hummingbirds

Hummingbird Feeding

The smallest birds in the world are hummingbirds. Some hummingbirds are only as long as one of your fingers. Hummingbirds are found only in North and South America. There are over 300 kinds of hummingbirds. Only about 10 kinds are found in the United States.

Hummingbirds are one of the few birds that can **hover,** or fly in one place. Hummingbirds can even fly backward, or straight up or down. Hummingbirds can fly so well because they can move their wings very fast. Some hummingbirds can move their wings 80 times every second!

Hummingbirds need a lot of energy to move so fast. They feed on nectar. Nectar is a sweet, high-energy liquid made inside many flowers. Hummingbirds hover when they feed on nectar. Their beaks are shaped to reach into flowers to get the nectar.

Many hummingbirds have bright red, green, or blue feathers. You can see the colors in sunlight. In the shade, hummingbirds look gray or brown.

Hummingbirds build nests in trees and bushes. Their nests are made from twigs, grass, and even spider webs. Most nests are only a few inches wide. Hummingbird eggs are about the size of a pea!

A. Answer True or False.

1. Hummingbirds feed on nectar. _____

2. Hummingbirds have bright feathers. _____

3. The largest birds in the world are hummingbirds. _____

4. Hummingbirds build nests on the ground. _____

5. Hummingbirds can fly backward. _____

6. Hummingbirds use their beaks to eat insects. _____

7. Hummingbird eggs are very large. _____

B. Use the words below to complete the sentences.

| bushes | feathers | hover |
| energy | feed | nectar |

1. A hummingbird can _____, or fly in one place.

2. A high-energy liquid made inside flowers is _____.

3. Hummingbirds build nests in trees and _____.

4. Hummingbirds have very colorful _____.

5. Hummingbirds hover when they _____.

6. Hummingbirds need a lot of _____ to move fast.

C. Use each word to write a sentence about hummingbirds.

1. hover _____

_____

2. nectar _____

_____

3. nest _____

_____

85

Woodpeckers

Woodpecker

Woodpeckers live all over the world. They can be found wherever there are trees. You can even find woodpeckers living in city parks or in your own backyard. The name "woodpecker" fits these birds. They make drumming sounds by pecking on wood.

Woodpeckers use their tough, sharp beaks to drill holes in trees to get at insects under the bark. The insects dig their way into the wood and feed on the tree. Without woodpeckers, many trees would have so many insect pests that they would die.

Woodpeckers have other adaptations that help them catch insects. Their strong legs and toes can hold onto the sides of trees. Their strong necks help them move their head back and forth. Woodpeckers also have long tongues that they use to pull insects out of the holes they drill in trees.

Woodpeckers come in all sizes. Some are as small as mice. Others are as big as cats. The male woodpecker often has red feathers on the top of its head. The female has white or black feathers instead.

Woodpeckers nest in holes in trees. They make the holes with their beaks. Owls and other birds often nest in old woodpecker holes. Squirrels and other animals also use them.

So the next time you hear a drumming sound coming from the trees, look around. You may see a woodpecker hard at work.

A. Write the letter for the correct answer.

1. A woodpecker uses its beak to _____.
   (a) eat seeds   (b) catch fish   (c) drill holes in trees

2. Woodpeckers eat _____.
   (a) fish   (b) seeds   (c) insects

3. Strong legs and toes help a woodpecker _____.
   (a) run fast   (b) jump   (c) hold onto the sides of trees

4. A woodpecker makes its nest in a _____.
   (a) bush   (b) cave   (c) hole in a tree

5. Woodpeckers help control the number of insects that _____.
   (a) cut down trees   (b) eat trees   (c) live in tree roots

B. Write the word or words that best finish each sentence.

1. Woodpeckers can be found wherever there are _____.

2. Woodpeckers use their tongues to _____
   _____.

3. Woodpeckers drill holes in trees to make nests and to find _____
   _____.

4. Woodpeckers have tough, sharp _____ to drill holes in wood.

5. Without woodpeckers, many trees would have so many insect pests

   that _____.

C. List two adaptations that help woodpeckers catch insects. _____

_____

_____

_____

_____

_____

_____

Mockingbirds

Mockingbird

Mockingbirds are found in most parts of the United States but are most common in the South. They are well known for their songs. Mockingbirds sing both during the day and at night.

Mockingbirds are named for their ability to mock, or copy, the sounds they hear. They can repeat the songs of many other birds. One scientist has reported a mockingbird that can imitate more than 50 bird songs in an hour. Some mockingbirds can even imitate the sounds of a tree frog, a cat's meow, a piano, or a squeaky door.

In a tree, a mockingbird looks all gray. But its wings have a patch of white. When a mockingbird flies, the white flashes as the bird flaps its wings.

In the spring, each male mockingbird finds a good place to nest. Then he sings to attract a female. He also sings to warn other males away. If other male mockingbirds come into the area, the males will fight.

A. Answer True or False.

1. Mockingbirds can imitate the songs of other birds. _____

2. Sometimes male mockingbirds fight. _____

3. Mockingbirds sing only in the morning. _____

B. Answer the question.

How did the mockingbird get its name? _____

_____

Part A

Read each sentence. Write <u>True</u> if the sentence is true. Write <u>False</u> if the sentence is false.

1. All birds have feathers. _____
2. All birds have webbed feet. _____
3. All birds are warm-blooded. _____
4. All birds nest in trees. _____

Part B

Write the name of the bird that matches each description. Choose from the names below.

chicken	hummingbird	pelican
duck	mockingbird	penguin
goose	owl	turkey
hawk	parrot	woodpecker

1. Males of this bird are called toms. _____
2. This bird feeds on nectar. _____
3. This bird can copy the songs of other birds. _____
4. This bird can see well at night. _____
5. This bird has a pouch of skin under its beak. _____
6. This bird can talk and is often kept as a pet. _____
7. This bird has a long neck and honks. _____
8. This bird quacks. _____
9. This bird is black and white and cannot fly. _____
10. This bird drills holes in trees to catch insects. _____
11. This carnivorous bird is smaller than an eagle. _____

Make a Bird Feeder

You Need

- field guide to birds

Feeder 1

- plastic gallon jug
- knife
- birdseed
- string

Feeder 2

- net bag
- suet
- string

1. Make one of the bird feeders. The pictures show you what to do. If you make Feeder 1, ask an adult to help you cut the openings.

2. Hang your feeder from a low tree branch or from a porch or balcony. Make sure it is in a place where you can watch it.

3. Keep a list of the birds that visit your feeder. If you don't know all their names, look in a field guide to birds.

4. Compare your list with those of your classmates. Make a class list of seed eaters and suet eaters. Do any birds eat both?

5. Are the seed eaters alike? Are the suet eaters alike? Use your field guide. Compare the sizes, beak shapes, or other characteristics of each group of birds.

Write the Answer

What did you find out about one group of birds?

_____

_____

_____

Fill in the circle in front of the word or phrase that best completes each sentence. The first one is done for you.

1. All birds
   ⓐ can swim.
   ⓑ can fly.
   ● have wings.

2. Birds that are carnivores are
   ⓐ ducks, geese, and owls.
   ⓑ owls, hawks, and eagles.
   ⓒ chickens and turkeys.

3. Birds that are domestic animals are
   ⓐ owls and woodpeckers.
   ⓑ hummingbirds and eagles.
   ⓒ chickens and turkeys.

4. Feathers help birds
   ⓐ fly, stay warm, and stay dry.
   ⓑ fly, walk, and eat.
   ⓒ fly, dig, and sing.

5. A sharp beak helps a hawk
   ⓐ cut and tear meat.
   ⓑ pick fruit and open seeds.
   ⓒ dig holes in trees.

6. A domestic animal is an animal that has been
   ⓐ hunted and shot.
   ⓑ protected by laws.
   ⓒ tamed by people.

Fill in the missing words.

7. Birds are _____-blooded vertebrates.
   (warm, cold)

8. A _____ is a bird that has webbed feet.
   (duck, hawk)

9. Birds that eat fruit and seeds are _____.
   (hawks, parrots)

Write the answer on the lines.

10. Why do some ducks and geese fly south in the winter?

   _____

   _____

   _____

UNIT 6
Mammals

Elephants and people are mammals.

A dolphin is a water mammal.

What Is a Mammal?

There are more than 4,000 different kinds of **mammals.** Cats, dogs, and farm animals are some mammals that are familiar to you. Other mammals, such as kangaroos and elephants, you may have seen in zoos. Then there are the mammals you see all around you. People are mammals, too.

What are mammals? Mammals are vertebrates. They have backbones, like the amphibians, reptiles, and birds you have read about. Mammals are also warm-blooded like birds. Their body temperature stays the same whether the outside temperature is hot or cold. Also, mammals breathe air with lungs. So do birds, reptiles, and most adult amphibians.

But mammals are different from other vertebrates in several ways. Most young mammals develop inside their mothers and are born alive. Young mammals feed on milk made in their mothers' body. Adult mammals protect and teach their young more than other vertebrates do. Mammals have hair or fur that keeps them warm. They also have brains that are more developed than the brains of other vertebrates.

Most mammals live on land and have legs to help them move. Bats are mammals with wings. They are the only mammals that can fly. Some mammals live in trees. Others live underground. A few mammals, such as whales and dolphins, live in water.

A. Write the letter for the correct answer.

1. Dogs, lions, and people are _____.
   (a) amphibians   (b) mammals   (c) reptiles

2. Mammals are _____.
   (a) vertebrates   (b) cold-blooded   (c) invertebrates

3. Mammals breathe air with _____.
   (a) skin   (b) lungs   (c) gills

4. Mammals have _____ that keeps them warm.
   (a) scales   (b) feathers   (c) hair or fur

5. Most mammals _____.
   (a) live on land   (b) fly   (c) live in water

B. Answer True or False.

1. Mammals do not have backbones. _____

2. The brains of mammals are more developed than the brains of other vertebrates. _____

3. Most mammals hatch from eggs. _____

4. Young mammals feed on milk made in their mothers' body. _____

5. Adult mammals protect and teach their young. _____

C. Answer the questions.

1. In at least three ways, mammals are like some other vertebrates. What are two of the ways? _____

   _____

2. How are young mammals different from other vertebrates? _____

   _____

   _____

Kangaroos

Kangaroo Hopping

Kangaroo and Joey

Kangaroos are mammals with short brown or gray fur. There are many kinds of kangaroos. Some are as small as a rabbit. The largest kangaroos are the great gray kangaroo and the red kangaroo. The males can grow to be more than 7 feet tall. Females are shorter.

All kangaroos have long back legs and short front legs. They move by hopping. Large kangaroos can hop up to 40 miles an hour. With their speed and ability to hop, they can get away from enemies. Kangaroos have long tails that they use for balance.

Most kangaroos live in Australia. Some live in deserts, some on grasslands, and some even live in trees. Kangaroos eat plants or grass. Sometimes they eat the grass that is food for cattle and sheep. Then farmers who raise cattle and sheep may try to kill the kangaroos.

Kangaroos belong to a group of **pouched mammals**. Females have pouches on their stomachs where they raise their young. The young are called joeys. When a joey is born, it is about 1 inch long. As soon as it is born, the joey crawls into its mother's pouch. It feeds on its mother's milk. After a few months, it can hop around on its own. But it will hop back into the pouch if it is scared. The joey finally leaves the pouch when it is about 8 months old. Within a day after it leaves, the female gives birth to another joey. A female never has more than one joey in her pouch at one time.

A. Use the words below to complete the sentences.

balance	hopping	milk
enemies	joeys	months
grass	kangaroos	pouched

1. Mammals that have long back legs and short front legs are

   _____.

2. Kangaroos move by _____.

3. Kangaroos use their speed and their ability to hop to get away

   from _____.

4. Kangaroos have long tails that they use for _____.

5. Sometimes, kangaroos eat the _____ that is food for
   cattle and sheep.

6. Kangaroos belong to a group of _____ mammals.

7. The young of kangaroos are called _____.

8. While in its mother's pouch, a joey feeds on its mother's

   _____.

9. A joey leaves the pouch when it is 8 _____ old.

B. Use each word to write a sentence about kangaroos.

1. pouch _____

   _____

2. hop _____

   _____

3. joey _____

   _____

4. legs _____

   _____

Bats

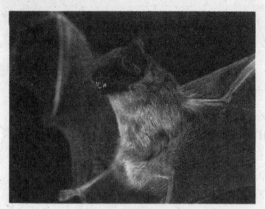
Bat with Wings Open

Bat Resting

Bats are the only mammals that can fly. The wings on a bat's furry body work like a bird's wings. But a bat's wings are covered with skin, rather than feathers.

Bats sleep during the day. At night, they fly around hunting for food. The most common kinds of bats eat insects. These insect-eating bats are the size of a mouse. Other bats that eat plants or fruit can be as large as a cat. Most fruit-eating bats are found in Africa or Asia.

The vampire bats in Mexico and South America are small. They use two sharp front teeth to bite sleeping animals. Then they feed on the animal's blood. The bite may not hurt the animal. But vampire bats can carry a disease called rabies. They can give the disease to other animals when they bite them.

Most bats can see well, but they can hear even better. They use their hearing to help them move around and find food. A bat sends out high-pitched squeaks with its mouth. The sound bounces off objects and comes back to the bat. When the bat hears the echo, it can tell where objects are and how big they are.

During the day, bats hang upside down in dark caves or hollow trees. In high places, they are protected from animals that might eat them. Millions of bats may sleep in the same cave.

A. Underline the correct words.

1. The only mammals that can fly are (birds, bats).

2. Bats (hunt, sleep) at night.

3. Vampire bats feed on an animal's (meat, blood).

4. Bats use their (sense of smell, hearing) to help them move around and to find food.

5. When bats sleep, they (go under rocks, hang upside down).

6. Bats that eat insects are the size of a (mouse, cat).

B. Answer <u>True</u> or <u>False</u>.

1. A bat's wings are covered with feathers. _____

2. Vampire bats can carry a disease called rabies. _____

3. Bats can see better than they hear. _____

4. Bats hunt for food during the day. _____

5. The most common kinds of bats eat insects, but other bats eat

   plants or fruit. _____

6. Vampire bats do not have teeth. _____

7. Each bat finds its own cave to sleep in. _____

8. A bat's wings work like a bird's wings. _____

C. Answer the questions.

1. A bat sends out high-pitched squeaks with its mouth. How do these

   sounds help a bat? _____

   _____

   _____

2. Why do bats sleep in high places? _____

   _____

   _____

Apes

Gibbon

Chimpanzee

Orangutan

Gorilla

Apes belong to a group of mammals called **primates**. Primates include monkeys, apes, and people. There are four kinds of apes. They are gibbons, chimpanzees, orangutans, and gorillas.

Gibbons are the smallest apes. They usually live in pairs in the high mountain forests of Asia. Gibbons use their long arms to swing from tree to tree. They feed on leaves and fruit. They often walk on two legs along the tree branches as they feed.

Chimpanzees live together in small groups in Africa. Chimpanzees are very good climbers but also spend time on the ground. They eat fruit and other parts of plants. Wild chimpanzees sometimes use tools. For example, a chimpanzee may use a twig to gather insects to eat.

Orangutans are bigger than chimpanzees. They can be found in some forests of Asia. Orangutans live by themselves. They make nests out of branches and leaves to sleep in each night. During the day, they climb through trees, looking for fruit to eat.

Gorillas are the largest apes. They live in small groups in the forests of Africa. Gorillas eat grass, leaves, and fruit. They spend most of their time on the ground. At night, the females and young may sleep in tree nests. But tree branches may not be strong enough to hold large male gorillas. So they sleep on the ground. Gorillas look fierce. But they are actually shy, friendly animals.

A. Use the words below to complete the sentences.

apes	gorillas	orangutans
chimpanzees	mammals	people
gibbons	monkeys	primates

1. Apes belong to a group of mammals called _____.

2. Primates include _____, _____, and
   _____.

3. The four kinds of apes are _____, _____,
   _____, and _____.

B. Write gibbons, chimpanzees, orangutans, or gorillas to answer the questions.

1. Which apes live in pairs? _____

2. Which apes live by themselves? _____

3. Which apes live in groups? _____

4. Which apes are the largest? _____

5. Which apes are the smallest? _____

6. Which apes use tools? _____

C. Answer True or False.

1. Gibbons use their long arms to swing from tree to tree. _____

2. Chimpanzees eat fruit and other parts of plants. _____

3. Chimpanzees are bigger than orangutans. _____

4. Gorillas eat grass, leaves, and fruit. _____

5. Gibbons often walk on two legs along tree branches as they feed.
   _____

6. Orangutans may use a twig to gather insects to eat. _____

99

Rabbits and Hares

Cottontail

Jackrabbit

Rabbits are small, furry animals with long ears and a short fluffy tail. Because their back legs are longer than their front legs, rabbits move by hopping. Hares look like large rabbits. They usually have longer ears and legs.

Rabbits have four large front teeth that never stop growing. A rabbit wears down its teeth by chewing. All rabbits eat grass and other plants. Most live in grasslands and fields. Rabbits live in almost every part of the world.

Cottontails are small wild rabbits. They are common on farms and in wooded areas. They spend the day in thick bushes. At night, they go out to feed on grass.

Jackrabbits are really hares, not rabbits. They are found in grasslands and deserts of the west. Jackrabbits can run as fast as 45 miles an hour. They use their speed to outrun enemies.

Snowshoe rabbits are also hares. They live in the cold north. Their big feet help them move over the snow. In summer, snowshoe rabbits have brown fur. In fall, they lose this fur and grow white fur. White fur makes them hard to see against the snow.

A. Answer True or False.

1. Hares look like large rabbits. _____

2. Rabbits have four large front teeth that never stop growing. _____

3. Cottontails are really hares. _____

4. Jackrabbits use their speed to outrun enemies. _____

5. Snowshoe rabbits live in the cold north. _____

B.

1. Rabbits move	common on farms and in wooded areas.
2. Cottontails are	in almost every part of the world.
3. Hares are	by hopping.
4. Rabbits live	larger than rabbits.
5. Snowshoe rabbits have	brown fur in the summer.

C. Answer the questions.

1. What are two differences between hares and rabbits? _____ _____ _____

2. What do all rabbits eat? _____ _____

3. When do cottontails usually feed? _____

D. Use each word to write a sentence about rabbits and hares.

1. ears _____ _____

2. legs _____ _____

101

Mice and Rats

Mice

Rat

Mice and rats belong to a group of small mammals called **rodents**. There are more kinds of rodents than any other kind of mammal. Squirrels, hamsters, beavers, and porcupines are rodents. The most common rodents are mice and rats.

All rodents have two big front teeth. The teeth never stop growing. Rodents must chew to keep their teeth short. Their teeth are well suited for gnawing, or biting on something for a long time.

Mice and rats both have pointed noses, big ears, and long tails. The easiest way to tell a rat from a mouse is by size. Mice are very small. Rats are bigger than mice.

House mice and rats live near people. They are often found in houses and barns. They can eat many different things. They like seeds and grain but can also live on garbage. House mice and rats will even eat leather, soap, and glue. House mice can cause a lot of damage by chewing on books and wires. Rats are bigger and stronger. They can cause even more damage than mice. Both rats and mice can carry insects that cause diseases.

There are many mice found in the wild. Because these mice are very shy and go out only at night, most people never see them. Wild mice rarely go into houses. Foxes, hawks, owls, and some other animals hunt wild mice for food.

Scientists often use mice and rats in their research to test new drugs and learn about diseases. What they learn can help doctors treat people who are sick.

A. Write mouse, rat, or both to answer the questions.

1. Which mammal is a rodent? _____

2. Which mammal has teeth that never stop growing? _____

3. Which mammal is smaller? _____

4. Which mammal can cause more damage? _____

5. Which mammal can carry insects that cause diseases? _____

6. Which mammal is stronger? _____

B. Answer True or False.

1. A rat and a mouse are the same animal. _____

2. A squirrel is a rodent. _____

3. There are many mice found in the wild. _____

4. House mice eat only seeds. _____

5. There are more kinds of rodents than any other kind of mammal.

   _____

6. House mice and rats can live on garbage. _____

7. The most common rodents are mice and rats. _____

8. House mice and rats rarely go into houses. _____

C. Answer the questions.

1. Why do most people never see wild mice? _____

   _____

2. What do house mice eat? _____

   _____

   _____

3. How are rats different from house mice? _____

   _____

The Cat Family

Pet Cats

Cats can catch mice and birds.

Have you ever had a cat for a pet? A pet cat belongs to a family that includes tigers, lions, and leopards. What does a pet cat have in common with these large, wild animals?

All cats have sharp teeth and claws. Cats use their teeth and claws to catch animals for food. Small cats can catch small animals like mice and birds. Larger cats, like tigers and lions, hunt deer and antelope for food.

All cats have tails and whiskers. The tail helps a cat keep its balance. When a cat is falling, it uses its tail to turn its body so it lands on its feet. Whiskers are the long stiff hairs that grow on the sides of a cat's face. They help give a cat a sense of touch. Cats can see well in dim light. Their eyes have a special lining that reflects light to help them see. The lining also makes a cat's eyes glow green when light shines on them at night.

Cats have soft pads on the bottoms of their feet. These pads help cats move quietly. Cats can run, jump, and climb trees quickly. Being fast and quiet helps cats to be good hunters.

Cats have been domesticated, or tamed by people, for almost 5,000 years. Ancient Egyptians thought that cats were special spirits.

A. Write the letter for the correct answer.

1. All cats have sharp teeth and _____.
   (a) feathers   (b) claws   (c) scales

2. A cat's _____ help give it a sense of touch.
   (a) whiskers   (b) tail   (c) claws

3. Cats have soft pads on the bottom of their _____.
   (a) tails   (b) heads   (c) feet

4. Being fast and quiet helps cats to be good _____.
   (a) pets   (b) hunters   (c) prey

5. Cats have been tamed by _____ for almost 5,000 years.
   (a) people   (b) dogs   (c) wild animals

B. Answer True or False.

1. Cats cannot see well in dim light. _____

2. A pet cat belongs to a family that includes tigers, lions, and leopards. _____

3. The tail helps a cat keep its balance. _____

4. Cats can run, jump, and climb trees quickly. _____

5. Being fast and quiet helps cats be good hunters. _____

6. Cats use their tails to catch animals for food. _____

7. Small cats can catch animals like mice and birds. _____

C. Answer the questions.

1. How do cats use their claws and teeth? _____

   _____

   _____

2. What are two reasons why cats are good hunters? _____

   _____

   _____

105

The Cat Family

Big Cats

Tiger

Lion

Leopard

Big cats live in many parts of the world. Tigers, the largest members of the cat family, are found in Asia. They have black stripes on their brownish orange fur. Tigers hunt alone in the forests. They eat large animals like deer and wild pigs. Tigers are one of the few cats that like to swim.

Lions are found mainly in Africa. They are the only cats that live in groups. These groups are called **prides.** A pride of lions can catch zebras, antelopes, and even young elephants.

Leopards, jaguars, and cheetahs are smaller than tigers and lions. Leopards live in Africa and Asia. Their yellowish fur has black spots. Sometimes a leopard is all black. These black leopards are also called panthers. Leopards are good climbers. They leap from trees to attack almost any kind of animal.

Jaguars are found in South America. A jaguar's fur has black circles with spots inside. Like leopards, jaguars spend much of their day in trees. They hunt on the ground at night. Jaguars will eat most animals, including deer, monkeys, fish, and even alligators.

Cheetahs are found in Africa and Asia. They have black spots on their fur. Cheetahs are the fastest land animals over short distances. They can run at speeds of more than 60 miles an hour.

Big cats have been hunted for their fur. Today most big cats are in national parks and game preserves. Some are in zoos.

A. Draw a line to match the big cat with its description.

1. lion   black circles with spots inside

2. tiger   fastest land animal over short distances

3. jaguar   lives in groups called prides

4. leopard   largest member of the cat family

5. cheetah   yellowish fur with black spots or all black

B. Use the words below to complete the sentences.

cheetahs   leopards   parks
fur   lions   tigers
jaguars   panthers   trees

1. Big cats that hunt alone in the forests are _____.

2. Good climbers that leap from trees to attack almost any kind of animal are _____.

3. Big cats have been hunted for their _____.

4. A pride is a group of _____.

5. Black leopards are also called _____.

6. Today, most big cats are in national _____ or game preserves.

7. Big cats that run more than 60 miles an hour are _____.

8. Leopards and jaguars spend much of their day in _____.

C. Use each word to write a sentence about big cats.

1. lions _____

_____

2. leopards _____

_____

The Dog Family

Pet Dogs

German Shepherd

Saint Bernard

Chihuahua

The dog family is very large. There are wild dogs and dogs people have as pets. The dog family is very large because there are hundreds of kinds of pet dogs. The dog was probably the first mammal to be domesticated, or trained to live with people. People may have had pet dogs 12,000 years ago. Today, people all over the world have pet dogs.

In certain ways, dogs vary. They vary in size and in shape. Their hair can be short or long. Their hair color can be black or white or different shades of brown.

But in many other ways, dogs are alike. Because they are carnivores, dogs have sharp teeth. They use their teeth to tear meat. Healthy dogs have cold, wet noses. They can smell and hear much better than people can. Dogs cannot see very well, but their other senses make up for their poor vision.

Domesticated dogs are not just pets. Some kinds of dogs, like collies, are guard dogs. They watch over sheep and cattle. German shepherds may guard houses. German shepherds are also used by blind people as guides, and by the police to sniff out drugs. Sporting dogs, like pointers, help hunters.

The Saint Bernard is one of the biggest dogs. It can weigh almost 200 pounds. The Saint Bernard has been used to find people lost in the mountains during snowstorms. The smallest pet dog, the chihuahua, may weigh only 1 pound.

A. Write the letter for the correct answer.

1. The dog family is large because there are hundreds of kinds

   of _____.
   (a) wild dogs   (b) pet dogs   (c) both wild and pet dogs

2. The first mammal to have been domesticated is the _____.
   (a) dog   (b) cat   (c) German shepherd dog

3. Dogs are _____.
   (a) herbivores   (b) carnivores   (c) omnivores

4. Dogs cannot _____ very well.
   (a) smell   (b) hear   (c) see

5. Sporting dogs _____.
   (a) guard houses   (b) help hunters   (c) guide blind people

6. One of the biggest dogs is the _____.
   (a) chihuahua   (b) collie   (c) Saint Bernard

B. Write the word that best finishes each sentence.

1. Today, people all over the world have pet _____.

2. Dogs use their sharp _____ to tear meat.

3. The chihuahua, which may weigh 1 pound, is the _____
   dog.

4. Dogs vary in size, in shape, and in the color of their _____.

5. Healthy dogs have cold, wet _____.

C. Answer True or False.

1. Some dogs, like German shepherds, are used by blind people as

   guides. _____

2. Saint Bernards are the smallest pet dogs. _____

3. Guard dogs, like collies, watch over sheep and cattle. _____

4. German shepherds are used by the police to sniff out drugs.

   _____

The Dog Family

Wild Dogs

Fox

Wolf

There are several different kinds of wild dogs. The largest wild dog is the wolf. A wolf looks very much like a large German shepherd. A wolf's fur is most often gray, but it can be white or black, too. Wolves live in groups called packs. Wolf packs eat almost any animal they can catch, such as deer. Wolves sometimes eat domestic animals, such as cattle or horses. Because of this, people often shoot wolves. Some people believe wolves attack people, but they do not.

Coyotes look like small wolves. Coyotes are found in many parts of the United States. They live alone or in pairs. They eat rabbits, mice, and dead animals.

Foxes look like small, thin dogs. Different kinds of foxes have different colored fur. But all foxes have bushy tails and long snouts. Foxes live throughout most of the world.

Dingoes are medium-size dogs found only in Australia. In the wild, dingoes howl instead of bark. Dingoes eat sheep and small kangaroos. The Australian government has tried to get rid of these wild dogs.

Jackals are wild dogs that look a lot like foxes. They feed on almost any small animal, but mostly on dead animals. Jackals are found mainly in Africa and Asia.

A. Write <u>wolves</u>, <u>coyotes</u>, <u>foxes</u>, <u>dingoes</u>, or <u>jackals</u> to answer the questions.

1. Which wild dogs look like small wolves? _____

2. Which wild dogs feed mostly on dead animals? _____

3. Which wild dogs live in groups called packs? _____

4. Which wild dogs howl, instead of bark? _____

5. Which wild dogs have bushy tails and long snouts? _____

6. Which wild dogs eat sheep and small kangaroos? _____

7. Which wild dogs look like large German shepherds? _____

B. Answer <u>True</u> or <u>False</u>.

1. Because dingoes are endangered, the Australian government is trying to protect them. _____

2. Foxes have bushy tails and long snouts. _____

3. Wolves attack people. _____

4. Coyotes live alone or in pairs. _____

5. Jackals will eat almost any small animal. _____

6. The different kinds of foxes all have the same colored fur.

_____

7. The largest wild dog is the wolf. _____

C. Use each word to write a sentence about wild dogs.

1. wolves _____

_____

2. foxes _____

_____

3. coyotes _____

_____

Bears

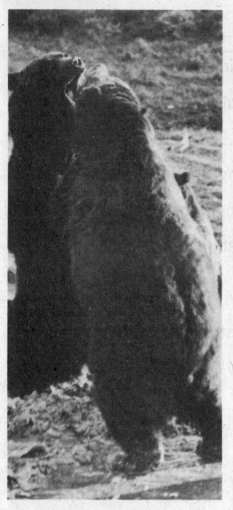

Grizzly Bears Fighting

Bears are large, heavy mammals with thick, shaggy fur. They have long claws and sharp teeth. Bears cannot see very well, but they have a good sense of smell.

Bears are omnivores. They eat mice, squirrels, and other small animals. But they also eat parts of plants, such as berries. They can open a beehive with their claws. Then they lap up the honey with their long tongues. Thick fur protects bears from bee stings.

Most bears hibernate in dens during the winter. A den might be in a cave or in a hollow log. Bears live off their fat while they sleep. Females give birth in the den. Baby bears are tiny and have no fur. But they grow fast as they feed on their mother's milk. In spring, the female and her young leave the den.

One of the largest bears is the grizzly, a kind of brown bear. A grizzly can grow to be 9 feet long. These huge animals spend their time looking for insects and berries. In the fall, many grizzly bears fish for salmon.

The black bear, the most common kind of bear, is smaller than a grizzly. It lives in forests in North America. It is very good at climbing trees.

The polar bear is found only in the Arctic. It is the best swimmer of all the bears. Its thick, white fur helps it stay warm. The pads of fur on the bottom of its feet help the bear walk on ice. A polar bear feeds on fish, seals, and walruses.

A. Write polar bear, black bear, or grizzly bear for each description.

1. the best swimmer of all bears _____

2. the most common bear _____

3. a bear that fishes for salmon _____

4. a bear that has thick, white fur _____

5. a bear that is good at climbing trees _____

6. a bear that eats fish, seals, and walruses _____

7. one of the largest bears _____

B. Answer True or False.

1. Bears have a good sense of smell. _____

2. All bears are carnivores. _____

3. Most bears hibernate. _____

4. Female bears give birth in the den. _____

5. Baby bears feed on berries. _____

6. A bear's den can be a cave or a hollow log. _____

7. Bears are covered with thick, shaggy fur. _____

8. All bears are the same size. _____

C. Answer the questions.

1. What helps a polar bear stay warm in the Arctic? _____

_____

2. What does a grizzly bear eat? _____

_____

3. How do bears get honey to eat? _____

_____

Elephants

African Elephant   Indian Elephant

Elephants are the largest land animals. Their trunks make them different from all other animals. The trunk is the elephant's nose. An elephant can use its trunk to pick up something as small as a peanut or as large as a log. An elephant also uses its trunk to drink water or to spray water or dust over its body.

Elephants live in groups called herds. They are herbivores. Elephants pull up grass or pick leaves from a tree with their trunks.

Elephants have two long teeth called tusks. Tusks are made of ivory. Some tusks can be more than 10 feet long. Elephants use their tusks to dig for food and to fight.

There are two kinds of elephants, African elephants and Indian elephants. African elephants are slightly larger than Indian elephants. They also have longer tusks and much bigger ears. African elephants have often been killed for their valuable ivory tusks.

Indian elephants are sometimes called Asian elephants. This is because they are found in other parts of Asia and not just India. Indian elephants are more easily led and managed. They are used to carry heavy loads and do other work. They are the kind of elephant usually used in circuses.

A. **Underline the correct words.**

1. Elephants are the (fastest, largest) land animals.

2. The trunk is the elephant's (tusk, nose).

3. Elephants live in groups called (prides, herds).

4. Elephants are (carnivores, herbivores).

5. Elephants have two long teeth called (trunks, tusks).

6. African elephants are slightly (larger, smaller) than Indian elephants.

B. **Use the words below to complete the sentences.**

African	Indian	tusks
fight	ivory	work
herds	trunk	

1. An elephant uses its _____ to spray water or dust over its body.

2. African elephants have been killed for their valuable _____.

3. The elephants usually used in circuses are _____ elephants.

4. Elephants use their tusks to _____.

5. The elephants with bigger ears are _____ elephants.

6. The tusks of elephants are made of _____.

7. Indian elephants are often used to do _____.

C. **Use each word to write a sentence about elephants.**

1. African _____

_____

2. Indian _____

_____

Deer

White-Tailed Deer

Deer are **hooved mammals.** Hooves are hard coverings over an animal's feet. Deer have long, thin legs that help them run fast and jump long distances. Pieces of bone, called antlers, grow on a deer's head. Antlers fall off in the winter, and new ones start to grow. Deer use them to fight and to defend themselves. Usually, only male deer have antlers.

Deer live in many parts of the world. Five kinds are found in North America. They are white-tailed deer, mule deer, moose, elk, and caribou.

White-tailed deer live in forests and meadows. They are more than 3 feet tall and have brownish hair. Their tails, which are white, give the deer their name. Mule deer look much like white-tailed deer, but their large ears are like those of a mule. Mule deer live in forests, deserts, and mountains of the west.

Moose are the largest deer. A moose can grow to more than 6 feet tall and weigh 1,000 pounds. Moose live in forests of the north. Like other deer, moose are herbivores. Often they go into lakes and ponds to find water plants to eat. Moose can swim very well.

Elk are the second largest deer. They live in mountains of the northwest. The males make a roaring sound to attract females and scare other males away.

Caribou live in the northern tundra, where no tall trees grow. In winter caribou migrate south in large herds in search of food. Caribou are often called reindeer.

A. Answer <u>True</u> or <u>False</u>.

1. Deer are hooved mammals. _____

2. Deer have long, thin legs that help them run fast and jump far. _____

3. Deer use antlers to fight and to defend themselves. _____

4. Moose are the smallest kind of deer. _____

5. Deer are herbivores. _____

6. Elk are the largest deer. _____

B. Use the words below to complete the sentences.

antlers	hooves	water plants
herbivores	tundra	

1. Pieces of bone growing from a deer's head are called _____.

2. The hard coverings over a deer's feet are _____.

3. Caribou live in the _____, where no tall trees grow.

4. Moose go into lakes and ponds to feed on _____.

C. Answer the questions.

1. Which kinds of deer live in North America? _____

_____

_____

2. Where are mule deer found? _____

_____

3. What do caribou do in winter? _____

_____

_____

117

Giraffes

Each giraffe has a different pattern of lines and patches.

The giraffe is the tallest animal in the world. The male, or bull, can grow to a height of 18 feet. The female, or cow, is shorter, but still taller than other animals. Giraffes have very long necks and legs. They also have hooves. Usually two small horns covered with skin grow from their heads. A giraffe's skin has orange or brownish patches with white lines between them. The color and pattern are different for each giraffe.

Giraffes are found in Africa. They live in grasslands dotted with trees. They use their long necks to reach tree leaves and twigs that they feed on. Giraffes use their long tongues, which they can stick out 18 inches, to pull leaves off trees.

With their long legs, giraffes can move very fast. If chased, they can run faster than 35 miles an hour. Most other animals are too small to bother giraffes. But sometimes a lion may chase them. Giraffes can usually outrun a lion. They can kill a lion with a kick of their front legs.

Giraffes have some problems because they are so tall. For example, they have trouble drinking water or eating grass. They have to spread their front legs far apart. Then they stretch their long necks down, keeping balance with their back legs. Giraffes also have a hard time lying down. They often rest and sometimes sleep while standing up.

Because giraffes seldom use their voice, some people think they cannot make sounds. But giraffes can make various sounds.

A. Write the letter for the correct answer.

1. The giraffe is the _____ animal in the world.
   (a) fastest   (b) tallest   (c) smallest

2. Giraffes have very long _____.
   (a) tails   (b) ears   (c) necks

3. Giraffes usually have two small _____ that grow from their heads.
   (a) tusks   (b) horns   (c) antlers

4. Giraffes use their long necks to reach _____ they feed on.
   (a) leaves   (b) small mammals   (c) birds

5. Giraffes have trouble _____.
   (a) running   (b) reaching tree leaves   (c) drinking water

6. Giraffes often rest while _____.
   (a) lying down   (b) swimming   (c) standing up

B. Answer the questions.

1. What is a male giraffe called? _____

2. What do giraffes eat? _____

3. What colors are giraffes? _____

_____

_____

4. How do giraffes protect themselves from lions? _____

_____

_____

C. Use each word to write a sentence about giraffes.

1. necks _____

_____

2. legs _____

_____

Camels

Two-Humped Camel

Camels Drinking

Camels are large hooved mammals. Camels were domesticated even before horses. For thousands of years, people have used camels for riding and as pack animals. They have also used camels for their milk, meat, and skin.

There are two kinds of camels. One kind has two humps and lives in the deserts and grasslands of Asia. The other kind has one hump and lives in Africa and Asia. People took one-humped camels to many parts of the world. One-humped camels were even used as pack animals in the western United States in the 1800s.

Camels are desert animals. They have many adaptations for living in the desert. Camels can go for a long time without drinking water. They can get much of their water from eating desert plants. They can eat thorny desert plants because their mouths have very thick skin. If there is no food or water, camels can live off the fat stored in their humps.

Camels have wide hooves that keep them from sinking into the desert sand. Their thick hooves keep the hot sand from burning their feet. Leathery pads on their knees allow them to kneel on the hot sand. Camels have long eyelashes that keep sand from blowing in their eyes. Also, their nostrils can close to keep out the sand.

A camel can carry heavy loads across the desert without stopping for water. No other animal is as helpful to people living in the desert as the camel.

A. Answer True or False.

1. Camels have hooves. _____

2. A camel never needs to drink water. _____

3. Camels can eat thorny desert plants. _____

4. There are two kinds of camels. _____

5. Camels are found only in the wild. _____

6. People use camels only for riding. _____

7. Camels are desert animals. _____

8. Camels store water in their humps. _____

B. Write the word or words that best finish each sentence.

1. A camel stores fat in its _____.

2. Wide hooves keep camels from _____.

3. Long eyelashes help a camel by _____.

4. Leathery pads on its knees allow a camel to _____.

5. Camels have many adaptations for living in the _____.

C. Answer the questions.

1. What are five ways that camels have been used by people? _____

   _____

   _____

   _____

   _____

   _____

2. How does a camel live when there is no food or water? _____

   _____

121

Rhinoceros

Rhinoceros

The rhinoceros, or rhino, is a large hooved mammal that lives in Africa and Asia. Of all land animals, only elephants weigh more than rhinos.

Rhinos have poor eyesight. But they have good hearing and a very good sense of smell.

Rhinos have thick skin with very little hair. They have one or two large horns on their noses. The horns begin to grow soon after a rhino is born. The horns continue to grow all during the life of the animal. Horns are made of hairs that grow tightly pressed together. Rhinos use their horns to defend themselves. They also use them to dig up bushes and small trees. Then they feed on the leaves of the plants.

People have hunted rhinoceroses for their horns. So today, there are few rhinos left. But now there are laws to protect the ones that remain.

A. **Fill in the missing words.**

1. Only _____ weigh more than rhinos. (elephants, giraffes)

2. The horns of a rhino are made of _____. (bone, hair)

3. Rhinos feed on _____. (animals, plants)

4. A rhino uses its horns to dig up _____. (bushes and trees, small animals)

B. **Answer the question.**

Why are there only a few rhinos left? _____

_____

Part A

Read each sentence. Write <u>True</u> if the sentence is true. Write <u>False</u> if the sentence is false.

1. Tigers live in groups called prides. _____

2. Birds and mammals are both warm-blooded. _____

3. Deer have antlers that fall off in the winter. _____

4. Some camels have two humps. _____

5. There are no mammals that can fly. _____

6. The largest land animal is the elephant. _____

7. A fox is a very large wild dog. _____

8. Of all land animals, only elephants weigh more than rhinos. _____

9. Most bears are active during the winter. _____

Part B

Write the letter for the correct answer.

1. Apes belong to a group of mammals called _____.
   (a) primates   (b) carnivores   (c) amphibians

2. Kangaroos are _____ mammals.
   (a) cold-blooded   (b) pouched   (c) hooved

3. Rabbits are _____.
   (a) carnivores   (b) herbivores   (c) omnivores

4. The giraffe is the _____ animal in the world.
   (a) tallest   (b) slowest   (c) shortest

5. Elephants have long teeth called _____.
   (a) hooves   (b) antlers   (c) tusks

6. Mice and rats belong to a group of small mammals called _____.
   (a) rodents   (b) pouched animals   (c) domesticated animals

7. The cat family does not include _____.
   (a) lions   (b) tigers   (c) caribou

EXPLORE & DISCOVER

Take a Pet Survey

You Need
- drawing paper
- crayons or markers
- rulers

1. Work with your classmates. Have each student who has a pet animal write the kind of animal on the chalkboard.

2. Count how many there are of each kind of animal and write down the numbers.

3. Classify the pet animals as mammals, birds, reptiles, amphibians, or fish. You may also need the category *invertebrates*. Count how many pets belong in each category.

4. Make a large picture graph like the one shown here. Use your ruler to draw a grid on your drawing paper.

5. Draw animal pictures to show how many pets are in each category. (You could also use animal stickers or rubber stamps.)

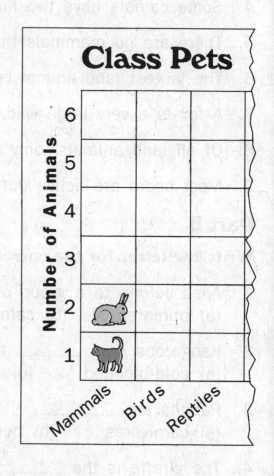

Write the Answer

Which category of pet animal is the most popular in your class? Why do you think this is?

_____

_____

_____

Fill in the circle in front of the word or phrase that best completes each sentence. The first one is done for you.

1. Because they are so tall, giraffes have trouble
   ⓐ reaching tree leaves.
   ⓑ outrunning lions.
   ● drinking water.

2. A domesticated mammal is the
   ⓐ wolf.
   ⓑ dog.
   ⓒ bear.

3. Two kinds of carnivorous animals are
   ⓐ camels and elephants.
   ⓑ rats and mice.
   ⓒ dogs and cats.

4. A wild cat that lives in groups called prides is a
   ⓐ lion.
   ⓑ leopard.
   ⓒ tiger.

5. Mice belong to a group called
   ⓐ rodents.
   ⓑ pouched animals.
   ⓒ hooved mammals.

6. An elephant is the only mammal with
   ⓐ hair.
   ⓑ a trunk.
   ⓒ four legs.

Fill in the missing words.

7. All mammals have _____. (backbones, tails)

8. A group of wolves is a _____. (herd, pack)

9. A mammal that flies is a _____. (bat, gibbon)

Write the answer on the lines.

10. What food do mammals feed their young?

_____

_____

_____

UNIT 7
Conservation

Dinosaur

Modern Horse

Dawn Horse

Extinct Animals

For 140 million years, huge reptiles called dinosaurs lived on Earth. Then, about 65 million years ago, they all died out. Dinosaurs became **extinct.** An animal becomes extinct when every one of its kind has died.

Since living things first appeared on Earth, some animals have become extinct. Over millions of years the land changed. The climate changed. Some kinds of animals could not survive the changes. Perhaps this was true of dinosaurs.

Not all animals died out as the land and climate changed. Some animals changed and were able to survive. These changes took millions of years.

About 55 million years ago, the **dawn horse** lived in North America and Europe. This horse was only about 10 to 20 inches high and it ate leaves. Slowly the land dried out and tall grasses began to grow. The dawn horse slowly began to change, too. It developed into a larger horse. Its teeth changed to chew grasses instead of leaves. Its feet changed to run over hard, dry ground. Horses of today are descendants of the dawn horse.

Changes that people make on Earth can cause animals to become extinct. When people take over the land where animals are found, animals have less space to live. They may not be able to find food. This is happening in the rain forests of Asia and South America. Without the help of people, animals like the orangutan and the jaguar may become extinct.

A. Answer True or False.

1. For 140 million years, huge reptiles called horses lived on Earth.
   _____

2. About 65 million years ago, dinosaurs became extinct. _____

3. An animal becomes extinct when every one of its kind is safe.
   _____

4. Since living things first appeared on Earth, some animals have become extinct. _____

B. Use the words below to complete the sentences.

climate	inches	millions
dawn horse	leaves	survive

Not all animals died out as the land and _____ changed. Some animals changed and were able to _____. These changes took _____ of years. About 55 million years ago, the _____ lived in North America and Europe. It was only about 10 to 20 _____ high and ate _____.

C. Answer the questions.

1. What happened to the dawn horse as the land began to change?

   _____

   _____

   _____

   _____

2. What happens when people take over the land where animals are found?

   _____

   _____

Endangered Animals

Bald Eagle

Bison

Some kinds of animals are being found on Earth in very small numbers. These animals are **endangered.** In other words, they may become extinct.

Remember that some animals can become endangered when people take over the land where the animals live. Other animals become endangered because they are hunted. Elephants, for example, are killed for their ivory tusks. Tigers are killed for their fur. Animals like the wolf and the grizzly bear are killed because they attack cows and sheep.

Some animals are harmed by chemicals that people add to the environment. The bald eagle is the national bird of the United States. It was harmed by a chemical called DDT. DDT was once used to kill insects. Fish and other animals ate the insects. Eagles ate these animals. The DDT got into the eagles' bodies. It caused them to lay eggs with thin shells. The eggs broke when the adults sat on the nest. Few new birds were born.

Chemicals like DDT are no longer allowed to be used in the United States. Birds like the bald eagle are able to reproduce once again.

Many American bison were once killed for their meat and fur. They were also hunted for sport. The bison became endangered. But laws were made to protect these animals. Then the number of bison began to increase.

People can sometimes be a threat to animals. But people can also help to protect animals from becoming extinct.

A. Fill in the missing words.

1. Animals that are being found in small numbers on Earth are _____. (safe, endangered)

2. Tigers are killed for their _____. (tusks, fur)

3. Some animals are harmed by _____ that people add to the environment. (chemicals, water)

4. Many American bison were once killed for their _____ and their fur. (tusks, meat)

B. Answer True or False.

1. The number of bison is becoming smaller. _____

2. The bald eagle was harmed by a chemical called DDT. _____

3. People can help protect animals from becoming extinct. _____

4. Animals that are endangered cannot become extinct. _____

C. The sentences below tell what happened to the bald eagle. Number the sentences in the correct order. The first one is done for you.

_____ Few new birds were born.

___1___ DDT was used to kill insects.

_____ The eagles ate these animals.

_____ The DDT got into the eagles' bodies.

_____ Fish and other animals ate the insects.

_____ The eggs broke when the adults sat on the nest.

_____ It caused the eagles to lay eggs with thin shells.

D. Answer the question.

Why are animals like the wolf and grizzly bear killed? _____

_____

_____

Protecting Endangered Animals

Whooping Cranes

Is anything being done for animals that are endangered? Many countries have laws to protect endangered animals. Also, breeding programs try to increase the number of animals that are born.

The United States has a law that makes it a crime to kill an endangered animal. The government cannot start a project, such as a dam, that could destroy the home of an endangered animal. The law also makes the government identify animals that may be endangered in the future.

Whooping cranes are large, endangered birds that stand about 5 feet tall. They have long legs and necks. Whooping cranes once lived in many parts of North America. In the late 1800s, as more people settled in the United States, the homes of whooping cranes were destroyed. By 1941, only about 15 birds were left. Then the birds became protected by law. Their nesting grounds were protected, too. Their numbers began to increase.

There was a special breeding program for whooping cranes. These birds lay two eggs but raise only one chick. Scientists took one egg from nests and raised the young birds. A new flock was begun in Florida where they live all year. Then another flock was raised in Wisconsin. The breeding program worked. At first, whooping cranes migrated only between Canada and Texas every year. Now whooping cranes fly between Wisconsin and Florida as well. In 2003, 320 whooping cranes lived in the wild and 134 lived in captivity. Scientists are on the way to saving these beautiful birds.

A. Answer <u>True</u> or <u>False</u>.

1. Many countries have laws to protect endangered animals.

   _____

2. Breeding programs try to decrease the number of animals that are born. _____

3. The United States has a law that makes it a crime to kill an endangered animal. _____

4. Whooping cranes are endangered birds. _____

B. Put a _____ next to the ways that laws help protect endangered animals.

_____ By law, the government cannot start a project that could destroy the home of an endangered animal.

_____ The law allows people to hunt endangered animals.

_____ The law makes the government identify animals that may be endangered in the future.

C. The sentences below show the steps in the breeding program for whooping cranes. Number the steps in the correct order. The first one is done for you.

_____ A flock of whooping cranes that was raised in Wisconsin migrates to Florida.

_____ Scientists raised the young birds.

___1___ One egg was taken from a whooping crane's nest.

_____ A new flock of whooping cranes was raised in Florida, where they live all year.

D. Answer the question.

What is being done for endangered animals? _____

_____

_____

Wildlife Conservation

A swan is released in a wildlife refuge, where it will be protected.

People need places to live. They need farms to grow their food. They need factories to make the products they use. They need roads to travel on. But animals need homes, too. They need places to find food and raise their young. How can people and animals share this planet?

People can try to save the environment of animals. Saving the natural things on Earth is called **conservation.** To conserve wildlife, areas of land are set aside so animals and their homes can be saved.

Today, there are more than 400 **national wildlife refuges** in the United States. These refuges are places where animals and their environments are protected by law.

The first wildlife refuge was Pelican Island, off the coast of Florida. It was set up in 1903 to protect brown pelicans that nest on the island.

Other wildlife refuges protect other endangered animals like the bald eagle, the timber wolf, and the whooping crane.

National parks and forests are other special areas that are set aside to help protect animals. In a national park, there may be beautiful waterfalls, lakes, or mountains. A **national forest** is where many different kinds of trees are protected. Both plants and animals are protected in national parks and forests. But people can also use these areas and enjoy nature.

Scientists study plants and animals in refuges, parks, and forests. Their work may help to save living things.

A. Use the words below to complete the sentences.

factories　　　　　　　　food　　　　　　　　roads
farms　　　　　　　　　live　　　　　　　　young

People need places to _____. They need _____ to grow their

food. They need _____ to make the products they use. They

need _____ to travel on. But animals need homes, too. They need

places to find _____ and to raise their _____.

B. Draw lines to match the special areas with their descriptions.

1. wildlife refuge　　　　　may have beautiful waterfalls, lakes, or
　　　　　　　　　　　　　mountains

2. national park　　　　　where many different kinds of trees are
　　　　　　　　　　　　　protected

3. national forest　　　　place where animals and their
　　　　　　　　　　　　　environments are protected by law

C. Answer <u>True</u> or <u>False</u>.

1. Saving the natural things on Earth is called conservation. _____

2. There are no national wildlife refuges in the United States.

　_____

3. Scientists study the plants and animals in refuges, parks, and

　forests. _____

4. Only plants are protected in national parks and forests. _____

D. Answer the question.

What are three animals that are protected in wildlife refuges? _____

_____

_____

133

Keeping a Balance

White-Tailed Deer

Endangered animals must be managed wisely. Their food sources and their homes must be protected. They have to be able to reproduce and raise their young. Then their numbers can increase, and they can survive on their own.

White-tailed deer were once rare in the eastern United States. Hunting these deer was not allowed. Today, the deer are back in large numbers. So hunters are allowed to kill a certain number of deer each year. Hunting is one way to keep animal populations in balance.

A **conservation department** in each state makes hunting laws. People pay the conservation department for a hunting license. The money is used to care for parks, forests, and refuges.

Conservation is important not only for hunters, but for all people. To save animals, people must support the laws we have. They must work to make new laws that protect animals and their environments.

Answer the question.

How can people save animals? _____

_____

_____

Part A

Use the words below to complete the sentences.

breeding	conservation	endangered
chemicals	conservation department	extinct

1. An animal becomes _____ when every one of its kind has died.

2. Animals that are being found on Earth in very small numbers are

   _____ .

3. Some animals are harmed by _____ that people add to the environment.

4. Special _____ programs try to increase the number of animals that are born.

5. Saving the natural things on Earth is called _____ .

6. A _____ in each state makes hunting laws.

Part B

Read each sentence. Write True if the sentence is True. Write False if the sentence is False.

1. Horses of today are descendants of the dinosaurs. _____

2. Changes that people make on Earth can cause animals to become

   extinct. _____

3. The bald eagle was harmed by DDT. _____

4. Elephants are killed for their ivory tusks. _____

5. Many countries have laws to protect endangered animals. _____

6. Animals can be killed in a wildlife refuge. _____

7. Hunting is one way to keep animal populations in balance. _____

Graph the Whooping Cranes

You Need

- **graph paper**
- **a pencil**

1. Make a line graph, like the one shown here, to show what has happened to the whooping crane population.

2. In 1870, about 1,000 whooping cranes lived in North America. After that, many cranes died from illness, hunting, and loss of their homes. Plot the 1870 population on your graph.

3. Wildlife parks were created in Canada and in the United States to help the cranes. They were safe places for the cranes. But by 1941, there were only 16 birds left. Plot the 1941 population.

4. In 1967, a captive breeding program was created. Cranes born in captivity are released into the wild. By 1995, there were about 160 wild birds and 140 captive birds. Plot the total 1995 population.

5. Connect the points on your graph.

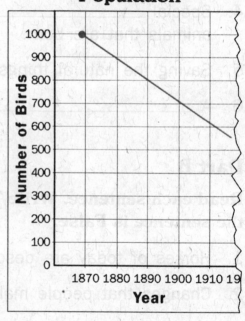

Whooping Crane Population

Write the Answer

Is the whooping crane population increasing or decreasing? Do you think these birds are still endangered? Why or why not?

_____

_____

_____

Fill in the circle in front of the word or phrase that best completes each sentence. The first one is done for you.

1. Horses of today are descendants of the
   ● dawn horse.
   ⓑ dinosaurs.
   ⓒ reptiles.

2. Animals found on Earth in small numbers are
   ⓐ extinct.
   ⓑ endangered.
   ⓒ safe.

3. Animals and their homes are protected in
   ⓐ farms.
   ⓑ factories.
   ⓒ wildlife refuges.

4. An endangered animal is the
   ⓐ whooping crane.
   ⓑ horse.
   ⓒ camel.

5. Saving natural things on Earth is called
   ⓐ hunting.
   ⓑ conservation.
   ⓒ reproducing.

6. To save animals people must
   ⓐ go hunting.
   ⓑ support laws that protect animals.
   ⓒ use DDT.

Fill in the missing words.

7. A _____ is an extinct animal. (dinosaur, bear)

8. The chemical DDT has harmed the _____.
   (elephant, bald eagle)

9. Endangered species can be protected by _____.
   (special laws, hunting)

Write the answer on the lines.

10. What are two ways that animals can become endangered?

   _____

   _____

   _____

A

adaptation, page 4.
An adaptation is a special body part that helps an animal live in its environment. An adaptation may help an animal get food or survive in hot or cold places. Some adaptations protect an animal from its enemies.

alligator, page 56.
An alligator is a large reptile that lives in lakes, rivers, or swamps. It has a large head, long tail, four short legs, and its body is covered with thick, hard scales.

amphibian, page 40.
An amphibian is a cold-blooded vertebrate animal that lays eggs in water. Frogs, toads, and salamanders are amphibians.

antennae, page 26.
Antennae are the feelers on top of an insect's head. An insect finds out what is around it by touching things with its antennae.

B

beak, page 8.
A beak is an adaptation that helps a bird get food. The shape and size of a beak can help tell you what the bird uses for food.

black widow, page 24.
The black widow is a kind of spider. The bite of the female is dangerous to people.

brown recluse, page 24.
The brown recluse is a kind of spider. The bite of this spider is dangerous to people.

burrow, page 14.
A burrow is a long hole in the ground made by prairie dogs. The prairie dogs sleep and store food in the burrow.

C

camouflage, page 12.
Camouflage is a protective coloring that helps an animal blend in with its environment.

carnivore, page 6.
A carnivore is an animal that eats other animals. Carnivores have adaptations, such as sharp teeth and claws, that help them catch their prey. Tigers, foxes, and eagles are carnivores.

caterpillar, page 34.
The wormlike stage of a butterfly or a moth is called a caterpillar. Caterpillars hatch from eggs. Their most important job is to eat. They feed mostly on leaves.

cocoon, page 34.
A cocoon is the silk covering that some caterpillars make. Caterpillars change into moths inside the cocoon. Most caterpillars that become butterflies do not make a cocoon.

cold-blooded, page 40.
Cold-blooded means an animal's body temperature changes as the outside temperature changes. Amphibians and reptiles are cold-blooded animals.

colony, pages 27, 72.
A colony is a large group of animals living together. Termites and pelicans are two animals that live in colonies.

comb, page 32.
A comb is a group of rooms in a beehive. The rooms have six sides and are made of wax.

compound eye, page 30.
A compound eye is one large eye made up of hundreds of tiny eyes. Compound eyes help ants see what is moving around them.

conservation, page 132.
Saving the natural things on Earth is called conservation.

conservation department, page 134.
A conservation department is an organization in each state that makes hunting laws. Conservation departments also take care of parks, forests, and refuges.

constrictor, page 60.
A constrictor is a large snake that wraps itself around an animal so the animal cannot breathe. Then it swallows the animal whole. The largest constrictors are the anaconda, the python, and the boa constrictor.

crocodile, page 54.
A crocodile is a large reptile with a long, flat body, four short legs, and a powerful tail.

D

dawn horse, page 126.
The dawn horse is an animal that lived about 55 million years ago. Horses of today are descendants of the dawn horse.

den, page 14.
A den is a hole in the ground made by a fox. The den protects the young foxes from other animals.

domestic animal, page 78.
A domestic animal is an animal that has been tamed by people. Chickens and turkeys are domestic animals. So are cats and dogs.

down, page 74.
Down is a layer of soft, thick feathers under the regular feathers of ducks and geese. Young ducks and geese are covered with down.

drone, page 32.
A drone is a male bee that mates with the queen bee.

E endangered, page 128.
Animals that are found in very small numbers are endangered. Unless they are protected, they may become extinct. The bald eagle is an endangered bird.

environment, page 4.
An environment is the place where an animal lives. An animal gets what it needs from its environment.

extinct, page 126.
An animal becomes extinct when every one of its kind has died. Huge reptiles called dinosaurs that once lived on Earth are extinct.

F fangs, page 62.
Fangs are the teeth that a snake uses to bite. A poison called venom goes through the fangs. Rattlesnakes and cottonmouths have fangs.

flock, page 68.
A flock is a group of birds living together. Many flocks of birds migrate during the winter.

G gills, page 40.
Gills are body parts that take air out of the water. Young amphibians are born with gills.

H herbivore, page 6.
An herbivore is an animal that eats only plants. Horses, deer, mice, rabbits, and elephants are herbivores. Herbivores have strong teeth to chew tough plant parts.

hibernation, page 10.
Hibernation is sleeping through the winter. Woodchucks and bears can't find food in the winter, so they hibernate in holes or caves.

hive, page 32.
A hive is a nest made by honeybees. It has many rooms with six sides.

honeybee, page 32.
A honeybee is the kind of bee that makes the honey and wax that people use.

hooved mammal, page 116.
A hooved mammal is an animal that has hooves, or hard coverings, over its feet. Deer, giraffes, camels, and rhinos are examples of hooved mammals.

hover, page 84.
To hover is to fly in one place. One of the few kinds of birds that can hover is the hummingbird.

I invertebrate, page 20.
An invertebrate is an animal that does not have a backbone. Worms, spiders, ants, and butterflies are examples of invertebrates.

K king, page 27.
The king is the male that mates with a queen in a termite colony.

L larvae, page 36.
The wormlike stages of life of some invertebrates, such as mosquitoes, are called larvae. Larvae hatch from eggs and grow into adult insects with wings.

lizard, page 64.
A lizard is a reptile with dry, scaly skin, four legs, and a tail. Lizards usually live in warm places, such as deserts. Most lizards hatch from eggs and can take care of themselves as soon as they are born.

lodge, page 14.
A lodge is a home that a beaver makes in the water. It is made from the trunks of trees.

M mammal, page 92.
A mammal is a warm-blooded vertebrate that breathes air with lungs. The young of mammals develop inside their mothers and are born alive. They feed on milk from their mother's body. Cats, dogs, and elephants are examples of mammals. People are mammals, too.

migrate, page 10.

To migrate is to travel to warmer areas to find food. Many kinds of birds that live in the north migrate to the south in the winter where it is warmer and they can find food.

migration, page 10.

Migration is traveling south to warmer areas to find food and returning north in the spring. Migration is a two-way trip.

mound, page 27.

A mound is a large nest made by a colony of termites.

N **national forest,** page 132.

A national forest is a place where many different kinds of trees are protected. Animals are also protected in national forests.

national park, page 132.

A national park is a special area that is set aside to help protect animals and plants. In a national park, there may be beautiful waterfalls, lakes, or mountains.

national wildlife refuge, page 132.

A national wildlife refuge is a place where animals and their environments are protected by law. National wildlife refuges protect endangered animals like the bald eagle, the timber wolf, and the whooping crane.

nectar, page 8.

Nectar is the sweet high-energy liquid made inside many flowers. Hummingbirds use their beaks to reach inside a flower to feed on nectar. Some bees collect nectar, which turns to honey in their stomachs.

nonpoisonous, page 58.

A nonpoisonous snake does not have poison in its bite.

O **omnivore,** page 6.

An omnivore is an animal that eats both plants and animals. Bears and raccoons are omnivores. So are most people.

P **pack,** page 16.

A pack is a large group of animals, such as wolves. All the adults in a pack feed and protect the young.

poisonous, page 62.

A poisonous snake has a poison called venom in its bite that can be dangerous to people. A person can get sick or die from the bite of these snakes. Rattlesnakes, cottonmouths, and coral snakes are some poisonous snakes.

pollen, page 32.

Pollen is a yellow powder that is made in a flower. Pollen helps flowers make seeds. As they feed, bees carry pollen from flower to flower, causing pollination.

pouched mammal, page 94.

A pouched mammal has a pouch on its stomach where the female raises its young. Kangaroos are pouched mammals.

prey, page 56.

Prey is an animal that is hunted and used for food by another animal. Fish, birds, and frogs are the prey of alligators.

pride, page 106.

A pride is a group of lions.

primates, page 98.

The primates are a group of mammals that include monkeys, apes, and people.

pupa, page 34.

The pupa is a stage in the life of a caterpillar. When its skin gets hard, the caterpillar becomes a pupa. It then grows wings and becomes an adult butterfly.

Q **queen,** page 27.

The queen is the female that lays eggs in an insect colony. The queen usually grows much larger than the other insects.

R **reproduce,** page 16.

When animals reproduce, they make more living things like themselves. Some animals reproduce by laying eggs. Others give birth to live young.

reptile, page 50.

A reptile is a cold-blooded vertebrate that breathes air with lungs. Most reptiles lay eggs on land. Their skin can be covered with scales or hard plates. Turtles, alligators, crocodiles, snakes, and lizards are reptiles.

rodent, page 102.

A rodent is a small mammal that has two large front teeth that never stop growing. Mice and rats are the most common rodents.

S **scales,** pages 34, 50.

The wings of butterflies and moths are covered with thin, featherlike scales. A reptile's body is covered with thin, hard scales that overlap.

scavenger, page 6.

A scavenger is an animal that eats only dead animals. A bird called a vulture is a scavenger.

shed, page 50.

Snakes shed, or get rid of, their skin in order to grow. Snakes shed their skin three to six times a year.

snake, page 58.

A snake is a reptile that does not have legs. It is covered with dry, tough scales. Snakes are carnivores with special jaws that allow their mouths to open very wide to swallow prey.

soaring, page 76.

Soaring is flying without flapping the wings. Eagles and hawks spend much of their time soaring.

soldier, page 27.

A soldier is an insect that protects a colony from enemies. There are soldiers in both termite colonies and ant colonies.

T **tadpole,** page 40.

A tadpole is a young frog or toad. It has gills and a tail, but no legs.

talons, page 76.

Talons are long, sharp claws. Birds like eagles and hawks use their talons to grab and hold their food.

tortoise, page 52.

A tortoise is a turtle that lives only on land. Tortoises like dry places. They can grow to be 14 inches long, larger than other land turtles.

turtle, page 52.

A turtle is a reptile with a shell made of hard, bony plates. Most turtles live in water and can grow to be very large.

V **venom,** page 62.

Venom is a poison that goes through the fangs of a snake.

vertebrate, page 20.

A vertebrate is an animal that has a backbone. People, horses, and cats are examples of vertebrates.

W **warm-blooded,** page 68.

The body temperature of a warm-blooded animal always stays the same. Birds and mammals are warm-blooded.

worker, page 27.

A worker is an insect that does all the work in an insect colony.

WONDERS OF SCIENCE

Acknowledgments

Illustrations

Alex Bloch—**8, 14, 20, 22, 28, 30, 32, 34L, 126**
Leslie Dunlap—**18, 38, 90, 124**
Kathie Kelleher—**T27, 48, 66**
Erika Kors—**54, 60, 64B**
Laurie O'Keefe—**72, 74, 76, 78B, 82, 88**
All Other Illustrations
Don Collins and Lewis Calver

Photographs

P.**4 (top)** © Holt Confer/Grant Heilman Photography; p.**6 (top)** © Grant Heilman Photography, **(bottom)** © Galen Rowell/Peter Arnold; p.**10** © Len Rue, Jr./Animals, Animals; p.**12** Wilfred Miller/American Museum of Natural History; p.**16** © Hans Pfletschinger/Peter Arnold; p.**24** F. Overton/American Museum of Natural History; p.**27 (top)** © Grant Heilman Photography, **(bottom)** American Museum of Natural History; p.**28** © Runk/Schoenberger/Grant Heilman Photography; p.**42 (bottom)** F. Overton/American Museum of Natural History; pp.**44, 46** © J. Kirschner/American Museum of Natural History; p.**50** © Philip Gould/CORBIS; p.**52 (top)** © Joel Sartore/Getty Images, **(bottom)** Zigheszczynski/Animals, Animals; p.**56** Carl Pucell; p.**58 (left)** Missouri Conservation Commission, **(right)** Stephen J. Kraseman/Peter Arnold American Museum of Natural History; p.**62** Texas Parks and Wildlife; p.**68 (top)** R.S. Virdee/Grant Heilman Photography, **(bottom)** © Grant Heilman Photography; p.**70** © Peter Arnold; p.**80 (bottom)** © Grant Heilman Photography; p.**84** © Hal Harrison/Grant Heilman Photography; p.**92 (top)** Andras Danes/Tony Stone Images, **(bottom)** ©Jean-Claude Lejeune/Stock Boston; p.**94 (top)** © Bruce Coleman, **(bottom)** New York Zoological Society; p.**96** © Runk/Schoenberger/Grant Heilman Photography; p.**100** Texas Parks and Wildlife; p.**102 (top)** Cooke Photographic; p.**104** © Bruce Coleman; p.**108 (top)** The Bettmann Archive, **(middle, bottom)** © Ron Kimball/Ron Kimball Stock; p.**110 (left)** Texas Parks and Wildlife, **(right)** © Bruce Coleman; p.**112** US Department of the Interior, National Park Service; p.**116** Tennessee Valley Authority; p.**118** © Cynthia Ellis; p.**120 (top)** New York Zoological Society, **(bottom)** © Giorgio Gualio/Bruce Coleman, Inc.; p.**128** Texas Parks and Wildlife; p.**130** © Marshall Prescott/Unicorn Stock Photos; p.**132** Third Coast Stock Source; p.**134** © Thomas Kitchin/Tom Stack & Associates.

Additional photography by Royalty-Free/CORBIS, PhotoDisc/Getty Royalty Free and Photos.com Royalty Free.